“Letters from that City . . .”

Os Justi Studies in Catholic Tradition

General Editor: Peter A. Kwasniewski

1 • *Disputed Questions on Papal Infallibility*
John P. Joy

2 • *Does* Traditionis Custodes *Pass the Juridical Rationality Test?*
Fr. Réginald-Marie Rivoire, F.S.V.F.

3 • *The Liturgy, the Family, and the Crisis of Modernity*
Joseph Shaw

4 • *Illusions of Reform: Responses to Cavadini, Healy, and Weinandy*
Edited by Peter A. Kwasniewski

5 • *The Triumph of Romanticism*
Fr. Gerard G. Steckler, S.J.

6 • *"Letters from that City . . .": A Guide to Holy Scripture for Students of Theology*
Fr. Thomas Crean, O.P.

“Letters from that City . . .”

A Guide to Holy Scripture for Students of Theology

Fr. Thomas Crean, O.P.

Lincoln, Nebraska

Os Justi Press
P.O. Box 21814
Lincoln, NE
osjustipress.com

Send inquiries to
info@osjustipress.com

ISBN 978-1-960711-30-4 (paperback)
ISBN 978-1-960711-29-8 (eBook)

Typesetting by Nora Malone
Cover design by Julian Kwasniewski
On the cover:
The Evangelist John and Wedric
miniature from Liessies Abbey, France
(Wikimedia Commons)

To the brothers of Chémeré-le-Roi,
in token of gratitude and fraternal esteem

De illa civitate unde peregrinamur,
litterae nobis venerunt.
Letters have come to us from that City
whose pilgrims we are.

St Augustine, *On Psalm 90*, Sermon 2.1

Contents

Preface

THIS SHORT BOOK is not a commentary on the contents of the Bible. Its object is the Bible taken formally rather than materially—that is, my aim is to show what we should believe about the Bible insofar as it is an inspired book or collection of books. In the first place, I seek to show what the Church believes about Holy Scripture, and what she has defined. In the second place, I seek to show what further things it is reasonable for a Catholic to hold.

I hope that this book may be useful especially to those who are studying theology as seminarians or for a degree, but I have written it also with a wider readership in mind.

St Dominic's Priory
London

1

Fittingness of Inspired Writings

No strict necessity requires that the word of God to man be written down. God could have ordained that it be communicated by speech alone, from one generation to another. We have no proof that it was put in writing before the time of Moses.[1]

Nevertheless, it was for many reasons fitting that God provide mankind with a written record of His word, especially as public revelation grew, and the number of accredited teachers multiplied. Revelation contains not only doctrines but also many histories and exhortations which support and illustrate these doctrines, which it would have required a constant moral miracle to preserve intact by oral transmission alone. Yet divine wisdom does not normally work miracles to achieve what may be done without them.

Again, men, conscious of their weakness, are accustomed by a kind of instinct to attempt the preservation of great truths by the use of some abiding material.

Again, it is in some way connatural to man to be taught by writings, as these appeal to sight, the most perfect of the senses, and serve his convenience, being portable.[2]

---

1 Ex. 17:14, 34:27; Deut. 31:24.

2 Cf. St Augustine, *Against Julian*, II.37: "God, as it pleases Him and He judges expedient, Himself distributes His stewards, faithful and

Again, a written record both reassures those taught that their teachers are not speaking from themselves, and humbles the teachers, lest they be elated by their office.

Again, to receive a letter from a friend makes a deeper impression on us than to have that same friend's words reported to us by an intermediary.

Finally, an inspired book, or some excerpt from it, may be liturgically venerated, as when the Church processes with and incenses the book of the gospels.

For all these reasons it was fitting that an inspired record exist of God's word to man.

---

few and excelling many others, in diverse ages, times and places. So you see them gathered from various periods and regions, from the East and the West, not at a place to which men are obliged to travel, but in a book which can travel to men." He is, however, speaking of his own book, not of the Bible.

2

Primary Author of Scripture

Working in secondary causes in accordance with their nature, God therefore moved prophets, apostles, and others to record that which He had taught them for the benefit of all. He has sent into the world seventy-two books,[3] like the seventy-two disciples who were sent on ahead to every place to which He was to come.[4] Together these books comprise Sacred Scripture.[5]

God is the primary author of Sacred Scripture in all its parts. This is affirmed, first, by revelation itself: "All scripture, inspired of God, is profitable to teach."[6] The word translated as "inspired

---

3 Counting Jeremiah and Lamentations as one; *CCC* 120.

4 Lk. 10:1 (Vg.).

5 Note however that just as the word "sacrament" has a wider and a stricter sense, so in the patristic and medieval period, the words *Scriptura sacra* or *divina pagina* were sometimes used more broadly, to include also "the Fathers, the conciliar canons, and even the pontifical decrees and (more rarely) the more outstanding treatises of theologians": Yves Congar, *Tradition and Traditions* (New York: MacMillan, 1966), 92, with references. St Thomas Aquinas notes this in his writing on the *Sentences* of Peter Lombard: "Here by 'Scripture' he means not the canon of the Bible but the sayings of the saints"; *Scriptum super Sententiis*, II, dist. 24, *expositio textus*.

6 2 Tim. 3:16. The verse may also be translated, "All Scripture is inspired of God and profitable," etc.

by God" is θεόπνευστος, literally, "God-breathed." Speaking of prophetic writings, but using words that apply to the scriptural writers in general, St Peter states: "Prophecy came not by the will of man at any time: but the holy men of God spoke, inspired by the Holy Ghost."[7] Here, the word translated as "inspired" is φερόμενοι, literally, "being carried."

The Church's tradition upholds the plenary divine inspiration of Scripture. Speaking of the mysteries of the incarnation and redemption, St Athanasius declares: "This text and that, and, in a word, the whole inspirited Scripture cries aloud concerning these things."[8] Pope Gregory the Great, writing to the imperial physician Theodorus, asks: "What is sacred Scripture but a kind of epistle of almighty God to His creature?"[9] Five hundred years later, his successor, Pope Leo IX, in his *Profession of Faith*, sent to the patriarch of Antioch, affirmed: "I believe in the almighty God and Lord, author [*auctorem*] of the New and the Old Testament, of the Law and the Prophets and the Apostles." The Council of Trent, in its *Decree on Sacred Books and Traditions*, refers to God as the "author [*auctor*] of all the books of the Old and New Testament."[10] The two subsequent ecumenical councils have repeated the phrase.[11]

An attempt is occasionally made to argue that "author" is not in this context a good translation of the Latin word "auctor," on

---

7 2 Pet. 1:21 (Vg.).

8 *On the Incarnation of the Word*, 33.

9 *Epistles*, IV. 31. For an abundance of patristic and later references, see Eugène Mangenot, "Inspiration de l'Écriture," in the *Dictionnaire de Théologie Catholique* (DTC).

10 Session IV.

11 First Vatican Council, *Dei Filius*, cap. 2; Second Vatican Council, *Dei Verbum* 11.

the ground that the latter term has a wider meaning.[12] In fact, while both the Latin and the English word can be used more generally for "cause," the Latin phrase *auctor libri* appears to be no more ambiguous than the English "author of a book": it means the one who directly causes the book to exist and thus makes himself responsible for the statements which it contains. "Everything which the inspired authors or sacred writers assert must be held as asserted by the Holy Spirit."[13] Hence all parts of Scripture enjoy equal authority.[14]

Summing up the tradition of the Church, the Dominican theologian Melchior Cano wrote:

> We are to confess that each and every thing that was published by the sacred authors, whether great or small, was dictated by the Holy Spirit. This is what we have received

---

[12] For example, Raymond Collins, in the *New Jerome Biblical Commentary*, states that the word means simply that God is the "ultimate source" of the biblical books, and that it does not ascribe "literary authorship" to Him; *New Jerome Biblical Commentary*, ed. R. Brown, J. Fitzmyer, and R. Murphy (Englewood Cliffs, NJ: Prentice Hall, 1990), "Inspiration," 65:31. Louis Billot refuted this opinion a life-time earlier, *De Inspiratione sacrae Scripturae* (Rome: St Joseph's Press, 1906), 31, n. 1. God is the "ultimate source" of all books whatsoever. The *New Jerome Biblical Commentary* and its 1968 predecessor *The Jerome Biblical Commentary* are curious works, in that in each case their editors are also their censors: in other words, Brown, Fitzmyer and Murphy, having produced their book, were charged by a bishop with judging whether or not it was doctrinally sound! A review of the later version is available online: John Young, "Destroying the Bible," www.ewtn.com/catholicism/library/destroying-the-bible-12293.

[13] *Dei Verbum* 11.

[14] St Augustine, for example, speaks of "the Acts of the Apostles, joined to the gospels with equal authority"; *Against the Fundamental Epistle of the Manicheans*, 10.

> from the Fathers; this is impressed and as it were engraved on the minds of the faithful; and this is what we also must maintain, especially as the Church so teaches.[15]

For this reason, Holy Scripture is rightly referred to as *the written word of God.* Pope Clement I told the Corinthians: "Look carefully into the Scriptures, which are the true utterances (ῥήσεις) of the Holy Spirit" (45). St Cyril of Jerusalem instructed his catechumens in similar terms: "The Holy Ghost Himself spoke (ἐλάλησε) the Scriptures."[16]

The Scriptures are referred to as the *written* word of God rather than simply as "the word of God" since He did not constitute the deposit of faith simply by inspiring writers but also by instructing prophets and apostles, whom He inspired to declare His message by both the spoken and the written word. "Hold the traditions which you have learned," said St Paul, "whether by word or by our epistle."[17]

The Scriptures are called the word of God not only "objectively" inasmuch as, like the Nicene creed or the creed of Pope Pius IV, they contain only things revealed by God, but also "formally," in that God has expressed Himself to man *by causing them to exist*, with the result that they contain all and only that which God willed to express in this way.[18] Hence, the Fathers of Vatican I expressly taught that the biblical books are not called

[15] *De locis theologicis*, II.17.

[16] *Catechetical Lectures*, 16.2. St Irenaeus, likewise, declared that Christians must be confident that the Scriptures are perfect (*perfectae*), "since they were spoken by the Word of God and His Spirit" (*Adversus haereses*, 2.28).

[17] 2 Thess. 2:14. This fact is generally denied by Protestantism, which tends to use "the Bible" and "the word of God" as synonyms.

[18] *Dei Verbum* 24 suggests both senses: "The Sacred Scriptures contain the word of God and since they are inspired, really are the word of God."

"sacred and canonical" simply because they contain revelation without error, or as if "having been composed by human industry alone, they had afterwards been confirmed by her [the Church's] authority,"[19] but because "having been written by the inspiration of the Holy Spirit, they have God for their author."[20] It therefore anathematised anyone who might deny that they are divinely inspired (*divinitus inspiratos*), "entire and with all their parts."[21]

Despite these clear assertions, some Catholic writers have claimed that only certain categories of scriptural statements are inspired, for example those pertaining directly to faith or morals.[22] The popes have therefore felt obliged to reject this error explicitly. Leo XIII, in *Providentissimus Deus* (1893), described this opinion as entirely impious, *nefas omnino*, and Pope Benedict XV repeated his words in *Spiritus Paraclitus* (1920).[23] Pope Pius XII

---

[19] This suggestion had been made by Daniel Haneberg (1816–1876).

[20] *Dei Filius*, ch. 2.

[21] Ibid., canon 4.

[22] St John Henry Newman favoured this position in his short work *What Is of Obligation for a Catholic to Believe Concerning the Inspiration of the Canonical Scriptures?* (London: Burns and Oates, 1884). He suggested that just as someone can be in a state of grace and yet commit venial sins, so the scriptural authors could have been continually inspired and yet have committed minor errors of fact that did not impede the message that God willed to convey to mankind. The mistake here lies in thinking of inspiration as a habitual gift rather than as a present act of God. Just as no one can sin insofar as he is moved by God, so no one can err insofar as he is inspired by God. It is strange to find the great Newman writing as a forerunner of the *Jerome Biblical Commentary*. One is reminded of some words of Chesterton, that many forerunners would have felt rather ill had they seen some of the things that they foreran.

[23] For the exercise of the infallible magisterium in *Providentissimus Deus*, see John P. Joy, *Disputed Questions on Papal Infallibility* (Lincoln, NE: Os Justi Press, 2022), 86–92.

also repeated the condemnation in *Divino Afflante Spiritu* (1943) and *Humani Generis* (1950). Since it has nevertheless proved a stubborn error, it may need to be anathematized in set terms by the next ecumenical council.

3

Human Authors

THE DOCTRINE OF DIVINE INSPIRATION does not exclude but rather implies the truth that certain human beings were also the authors of the scriptural books. Human beings are true but instrumental authors of Holy Scripture. They are true authors, since that which they wrote proceeded not only from their hands, but also from their minds and wills. They are instrumental authors, since their minds and wills themselves were used by God as means to express His message.

Inspiration must be distinguished from merely material or external dictation, by which one person tells another what words he must write, without acting on that person interiorly. Such dictation, which is the only kind that one human being gives to another, does not cause the second person to be an author, but only a secretary.[24] We do not call a letter by the name of the secretary to whom it was dictated, whereas we do speak, for example, of

[24] It is apparently such external dictation that the founder of Islam claimed to have received from a violent spirit. By contrast, St Jerome, writing of the prophets of the Old Testament, says: "It was not that air, struck by a voice, reached their ears: rather, God spoke in the mind (*loquebatur in animo*) of the prophets, according to what another prophet says, *The angel who was speaking in me*" (*Prologue to the Commentary on Isaiah*, with final quotation from Zech. 1:9).

the epistle of *St Paul* to the Romans. However, inspiration, acting upon faculties higher than can be reached by men, may be called *divine* dictation.[25]

What then is biblical inspiration? The question was debated extensively by Catholic theologians in the modern era, especially from the seventeenth to the early twentieth centuries.[26] We need not follow the twists and turns of the debate here, but may offer the following definition, which seems necessary to render justice to both the divine and the human authorship: inspiration means that God so moves the intellect and will of a human being that this latter shall, with a certainty exceeding the forces of nature, conceive and express a thought, intend to write it down, and execute this intention.

In so acting, God is therefore not necessarily revealing a new truth to the writer; He may be causing the writer to call to mind a truth which he already habitually knows. Yet in virtue of divine inspiration, this very truth is now known in a more perfect way. Hence, St Thomas speaks of an intellectual light which may be "divinely infused into someone not so that he may know some supernatural things, but to judge, with the certainty of divine truth, about some things which can be known by human reason." Likewise, speaking of those Old Testament writers who are not reckoned among the prophets, he notes that while they often wrote of such humanly knowable things, they spoke "with the help, nevertheless, of divine light."[27] If it were not for such divine

[25] The Council of Trent uses the verb *dictare* to describe the action of the Holy Ghost upon the apostles; Session IV, *Decree on Sacred Books and Traditions*.

[26] For a very detailed account, see DTC, vol. 7, pt. 2, "Inspiration de l'Écriture," II. Nature; III. Étendue.

[27] *Summa theol.* II-II, Q. 174, art. 2, ad 3.

light, it would not be possible to distinguish God's action on the inspired author's intellect from His action as first cause on the intellect of any person conceiving a true thought. Thus, someone who composes a diary may fill it entirely with true statements, and he could neither think nor write any of them without the universal causality of God: yet his diary is not thereby inspired, nor is God its author.

Hence, inspiration cannot be reduced to mere "negative assistance," as if God's relation to the biblical authors differed from His relation to other authors only in that He willed to prevent them from thinking or writing anything other than that which He willed and therefore intervened if they did so;[28] for this would not suffice to make God the *primary* author of Scripture.

Should inspiration be considered a form of prophecy? Prophecy in the fullest sense is a divine gift by which God teaches a man that which he could not otherwise know.[29] As such, it sometimes precedes the gift of inspiration, but need not do so. For example, St John in the Apocalypse was first given prophetic knowledge of future events and then commanded and inspired to record them, whereas other biblical writers gathered their information by ordinary human means, as St Luke affirms of himself at the start of his gospel. Yet St Thomas states that "the mind of a prophet is instructed by God in two ways: both by an express revelation, and by a certain instinct, which human minds sometimes experience unbeknownst to themselves"; this latter instinct is "something imperfect in the genus of prophecy."[30] Again, since prophecy

[28] This was the suggestion of the Premonstratensian Johann Jahn (1750–1816).

[29] *Summa theol.* II-II, Q. 171, art. 1.

[30] *Summa theol.* II-II, Q. 171, art. 5.

consists more principally in the infusion of divine light for the purpose of judgement than in the infusion of information,[31] it appears that the gift of inspiration, without being prophecy in the full sense, nevertheless pertains to the category of prophecy: it is a light by which the writer judges with a more than human certainty about what he is to say, whether or not he is conscious of having received such a gift.

It is true that God may speak to mankind through a human being without enlightening him in any special way, and even while this human being misunderstands the meaning of his own words. This is presumably what happened when Caiaphas prophesied (ἐπροφήτευσεν) that it was necessary for one man to die for the people (Jn. 11:51). Is it possible that He acted sometimes in this way when speaking through the biblical authors? A contemporary theologian has made this suggestion, arguing that otherwise we should be obliged to accept as the divinely-intended meaning of Scripture certain things that are false or otherwise objectionable.[32] On this view, we may sometimes believe the Scriptures without believing the original human authors of the Scriptures.[33] This author argues that we nevertheless may accept "the traditional position that the meaning that God intends to communicate in the Scriptures is the meaning intended by their human authors,

---

[31] *Summa theol.* II-II, Q. 173, art. 2. This is because it is the act of judgement that perfects the process of knowledge (*est completivum cognitionis*).

[32] John Lamont, *Divine Faith* (New York and London: Routledge, 2016), 155. For example, "it is quite likely . . . that the author of Psalm 137 really meant to bless those who bashed out the brains of Babylonian children." St Thomas speaks in this way of the imprecatory psalms: "The prophets in the Scriptures sometimes call down evils on sinners, as it were conforming their will to divine justice, although such curses may also be understood as prophecies" (*Summa theol.* II-II, Q. 76, art. 1).

[33] Lamont, *Divine Faith*, 157, n12.

if it is understood that the human author of the Scriptures is the Church."[34]

One problem with this suggestion is that it does not seem to do justice to the great respect with which the Church has always spoken of the biblical authors: "the holy men of God spoke, inspired by the Holy Ghost" (2 Pet. 1:21).[35] It also seems to run contrary to the teaching of the Second Vatican Council that "everything that the inspired authors or sacred writers (*auctores inspirati seu hagiographi*) assert must be held to be asserted by the Holy Spirit" (*Dei Verbum* 11). It is the meaning of one's words that one asserts, not the bare words themselves. Finally, it also seems hard to reconcile with the teaching of the First Vatican Council, mentioned above, that the biblical books did not become sacred and canonical in virtue of something that the Church did after they had been written.

---

[34] Lamont, 176, n49.

[35] "Holy men of God" is the Vulgate reading; the Greek text according to the modern critical edition has "men of God."

4

Verbal Inspiration

In recent centuries, it has been discussed whether inspiration extends only to the meaning intended by the human author, or also to his very words.[36] Certainly it cannot extend only to the meaning in the sense of some general truth which the human author would then elaborates as he chose: as if God had simply inspired both St Peter and St Paul to teach the necessity of baptism, and the former had chosen to express this doctrine by the figure of the Ark, and the latter by the image of burial and resurrection. This would not be compatible with the divine authorship of Scripture "in all its parts." But does it follow that the words themselves must be given by God, in the same way as the meaning? A problem with this view is that translations of the Bible would then not be Holy Scripture except in an equivocal sense. On the other hand, it seems that in some sense divine inspiration must extend as far as the words themselves, since it is the biblical *books* which are inspired, and books consist of words and not thoughts. Hence Vatican I says that the books of the Bible are called "sacred and canonical" insofar as they were

[36] This question was agitated especially from the time of the Jesuit author Leonard Lessius (d. 1623). See *DTC*, vol. 7, pt. 2, "Inspiration de l'Écriture," II. Nature; III. Étendue.

written (*conscripti*) by the inspiration of the Holy Spirit.[37] Yet on this view, one will naturally wonder whence comes the difference in styles of the various sacred writers.

It is reasonable to suppose that divine inspiration may relate to the words in at least three ways. First, there are certainly cases, especially in the prophetic books, where words are directly given by God. The vocation of Jeremiah is typical: "The Lord put forth his hand, and touched my mouth: and the Lord said to me: Behold I have given my words in thy mouth" (Jer. 1:9).

Next, there are biblical books that depend upon human research and reflection, such as the Acts of the Apostles. Since it is connatural to man to think with words in his imagination, it follows that when he is thinking in this way and is enlightened by God to make a correct judgement, he makes it in words. These words may thus be said to be included secondarily and "materially" in his divinely enlightened judgement, while the preexisting differences of character and native idiom among the biblical writers sufficiently explain the difference of their linguistic styles. "A secondary, instrumental cause," writes St Thomas, "does not share in the action of the higher cause, except insofar as it

[37] *Dei Filius*, cap. 2. Similarly, Pius XII in *Divino Afflante Spiritu* wrote (no. 15): "It is the duty of the exegete to lay hold, so to speak, with the greatest care and reverence of the very least expressions which, under the inspiration of the divine Spirit, have flowed from the pen of the sacred writer (*minima quaeque, quae divino Flamine inspirante, ex hagiographi calamo prodiere*)." Cf. Melchior Cano, *De locis theologicis* II.17: "Since the law of Moses, which is the *ministry of death*, was written with such care and precision that not one jot or tittle could pass from it, much more certainly is the gospel of Christ, which is the *ministry of spirit and life* written with such care and such in-breathing of God's aid, that there is not only no word in it, but not even any tittle, which is not supplied by the Spirit of God."

performs something proper to itself which disposes the way to the effect of the principal cause."[38] Thus a pen has for its proper act the making of marks on paper, which disposes the way to the effect intended by a writer, namely the expressing of himself in writing by means of *these* marks. A human being has for his proper act the conceiving of thoughts with the help of words expressed in the imagination; when he becomes an instrument of the Holy Spirit, this proper act disposes the way to the effect intended by God, namely the expression of the divine thoughts through *these* human thoughts and words.[39]

Finally, it may be that God sometimes infused into the minds of the biblical writers some truth, which they themselves had to "translate" into their own imagination.[40] In such a case, inspiration would imply a guarantee that God will not permit the author to err in this process of translation.

38 *Summa theol.* 1, Q. 45, art. 5.

39 Cf. Billot, *De Inspiratione*, 51–54.

40 See *Summa theol.* II-II, Q. 174, art. 1, for the distinction between prophetic truths conveyed to the bodily senses, to the imagination, and to the intellect.

5

Inerrancy

Since Holy Scripture is the written word of God, who can neither deceive nor be deceived, it is immune from all error. Christ Himself declared that "Scripture cannot be broken (λυθῆναι)."[41] Since the meaning of a statement is that which it bears in the mind of the person who affirms it, all the statements affirmed by the scriptural writers are therefore true in the sense in which they understood them. This is normally referred to as the "literal sense" of Scripture, though it is compatible with the conscious use of metaphor or allegory on the part of the human author.[42] The exegete should not, however, interpret the literal sense of Scripture by means of allegory or metaphor unless this is necessary. St Robert Bellarmine remarks: "One should not have recourse to figures, and leave the proper sense of the words, except when some absurdity would otherwise follow."[43] To do otherwise, he

---

[41] Jn. 10:35. In the context, these words can also be understood to refer to the particular passage of Scripture that was in question, namely Ps. 81:6.

[42] For example, the allegory of the eagles in Ezekiel 31. Such allegories *within* the literal sense should not be confused with the three non-literal senses of Scripture, for which see Section 10, The Plurality of Senses.

[43] *Controversiae*, "On the Church Triumphant," Bk. 1, ch. 3. Leo XIII asserted the same principle in *Providentissimus Deus*.

remarks, would be like entering a house by the window when the door is open. Since a figurative use of some word is by definition secondary, it would be perverse to interpret the Scriptures, or indeed any work, in such a way if the author has given no indication that we should do so.

Since they taught the plenary inspiration of Scripture, the Fathers naturally also taught its inerrancy. St Justin Martyr writes: "If there is any Scripture which can be urged as apparently contrary to some other, then, since I am convinced that this can never really be so, I should rather confess that I do not understand its meaning."[44] St Gregory Nazianzen declared: "We who extend the accuracy (ἀκρίβεια) of the Spirit to the merest stroke and tittle, will never admit the impious assertion that even the smallest matters were written down and elaborated at haphazard by those who have recorded them."[45] St Augustine expanded on this theme in a letter to St Jerome:

> I have learned to yield this respect and honour only to the canonical books of Scripture: of these alone do I most firmly believe that the authors were completely free from error (*nullum . . . aliquid errasse*). And if in these writings I am perplexed by anything which appears to me opposed to truth, I do not hesitate to suppose that either the manuscript is faulty, or the translator has not caught the meaning of what was said, or I myself have failed to understand it.

[44] *Dialogue with Trypho*, 65.

[45] Oration 2.105; *PG* 35:504. For similar patristic teachings, see St Clement of Rome, *Letter to the Corinthians*, 45; St Hippolytus, *On Daniel*, 4.6 and *Against Artemon*, quoted in Eusebius of Caesarea, *Ecclesiastical History*, 5.28; St Epiphanius, *Panarion*, 70.7; and St Jerome, Letter 27.1, *To Marcella*.

> As to all other writings, in reading them, however great the superiority of the authors to myself in sanctity and learning, I do not accept their teaching as true on the mere ground of the opinion being held by them; but only because they have succeeded in convincing my judgment of its truth either by means of these canonical writings themselves, or by arguments addressed to my reason.[46]

Elsewhere, writing to the same recipient, the bishop of Hippo emphasized that God could not be supposed to have permitted errors to occur in the Scripture for the sake of some greater good:

> Most disastrous consequences must follow upon our believing that anything false is found in the sacred books: that is to say, that the men by whom the Scripture has been given to us, and committed to writing, put down in these books anything false. It is one question whether it may be at any time the duty of a good man to deceive; but it is another question whether it can have been the duty of a writer of Holy Scripture to deceive: nay, it is not another question — it is no question at all. For if you once admit into such a high sanctuary of authority one false statement as made in the way of duty, there will not be left a single sentence of those books which, if appearing to any one difficult in practice or hard to believe, may not by the same fatal rule be explained away, as a statement in which, intentionally, and under a sense of duty, the author declared what was not true.[47]

---

[46] Letter 82.3.

[47] Letter 28.3. The theory of "tacit or implicit citations," put forward by some authors at the start of the twentieth century, must be rejected

St Thomas Aquinas refers to the inerrancy of Scripture in several places. Having explained that the Fathers, although they expounded the Scriptures under the influence of the Holy Spirit, nevertheless said certain things fallibly by their own judgement, Thomas pointedly adds: "This, however, must be held: that whatever is contained in Sacred Scripture is true."[48] Commenting on the opinion of certain Greek writers who had claimed that St John corrected the earlier evangelists about the date of Passover in the year of Christ's death, the Angelic Doctor writes: "It is heretical to say that something false in found, not only in the gospels but in any of the canonical Scriptures, and so it is necessary to say that all the evangelists say the same, and disagree in nothing."[49]

The popes, likewise, have taught that it is a matter of faith that Scripture is free of all errors, not only in matters of faith and morals, but in all matters. Pope Pius X formally condemned the following proposition: "Divine inspiration does not extend to all of Sacred Scriptures so that it renders its parts, each and every one, free from every error."[50] Pius XII in *Divino Afflante Spiritu* described the attribution of any error to Scripture as entirely unlawful, *nefas omnino*. He went on, quoting from Leo XIII:

---

for the same reason. This theory held that the biblical authors, when apparently relating historical facts, were in fact quoting from uninspired documents, intending simply to relay the contents of these unknown documents and not to vouch for their accuracy. See *Responsio* of the Biblical Commission, February 13, 1905, Denzinger-Hünermann (hereafter DH), 3372, and Billot, *De Inspiratione*, 148ff. By contrast, if a biblical author makes it clear that he is reporting another's words, these words may contain errors; the description of the Roman constitution in 1 Macc. 8 seems like an example.

48 *Quaestiones Quodlibetales* XII, Q. 17, ad 1.

49 *Commentary on the Gospel of St John* XIII, lect. 1.

50 *Lamentabili Sane* 11.

Divine inspiration "not only is essentially incompatible with error, but excludes and rejects it as absolutely and necessarily as it is impossible that God Himself, the supreme Truth, can utter than which is not true. This is the ancient and constant faith of the Church."[51]

[51] *Divino Afflante Spiritu* 3; internal quotation from *Providentissimus Deus* 20. In no. 2 of the same letter, Pius XII described *Providentissimus Deus* as the principal norm, *princeps lex*, in biblical studies.

6

Dei Verbum 11

The Second Vatican Council's Dogmatic Constitution on Divine Revelation, *Dei Verbum*, refers to the just-quoted passage from *Divino Afflante Spiritu* in its definition of the historicity of the gospels.[52] Unfortunately, a common mistranslation of another passage in *Dei Verbum* 11 has tended nevertheless to rekindle the heresy of limited inerrancy. The passage reads as follows:

> Cum ergo omne id, quod auctores inspirati seu hagiographi asserunt, retineri debeat assertum a Spiritu Sancto, inde Scripturae libri veritatem, quam Deus nostrae salutis causa Litteris Sacris consignari voluit, firmiter, fideliter et sine errore docere profitendi sunt.

One semi-official translation of this passage renders it thus:

> Therefore, since everything asserted by the inspired authors or sacred writers must be held to be asserted by the Holy Spirit, it follows that the books of Scripture must be acknowledged as teaching solidly, faithfully and without error that truth which God wanted put into sacred writings for the sake of salvation.[53]

---

52 *Dei Verbum* 19.

53 This translation appears on the website of the Holy See.

This translation is misleading in two respects. First, it is incorrect to translate *Litteris sacris consignari*, as "to be put *into* sacred writings" (or, as in another common translation, "to be put into the sacred Scriptures"). The Latin verb *consignare* does not mean "put into" or "consign," but "write" or "record," and it is followed by an ablative, not a dative; in the present case, by an ablative of means. Hence the correct translation of this phrase is "to be recorded by means of the sacred Scriptures."[54] In this way, one avoids the suggestion of the Bible as a preexisting receptacle for saving truth, which might therefore contain other statements, neither true nor tending to salvation. Secondly, the phrase "that truth," instead of "the truth," as a rendering of the term *veritatem*, might suggest that Scripture also taught other truths, not relevant to our salvation, and not necessarily "solidly, faithfully, and without error." Hence a better translation of the passage is as follows:

> Therefore, since everything asserted by the inspired authors or sacred writers must be held to be asserted by the Holy Spirit, it follows that the books of Scripture must be acknowledged as teaching the truth, which God wanted to be recorded by means of sacred writings for the sake of our salvation, solidly, faithfully and without error.[55]

[54] A similar mistranslation is found in the Italian, French, and Spanish versions provided on the same Vatican website, where we find, respectively, *consegnare*, *consigner*, and *consignar*. For a fuller discussion of this point, see Brian Harrison, "Does Vatican Council II Allow for Errors in Sacred Scripture?," *Living Tradition* 145–46 (March–May 2010), available online at www.rtforum.org/lt/lt145-6.html.

[55] The omission of "our" in the English version seems to be simply an oversight.

Such fine points of translation are not necessarily small matters:

> I established the new and the old covenants, they came out of my mouth, and there is no falsehood in them because I am the truth. Accordingly, those who say that I am false and that Sacred Scripture is false will never see my face.[56]

[56] Words which St Bridget of Sweden recorded as having been spoken to her by Christ: *Liber Caelestis* I.15, in *The Revelations of St Birgitta of Sweden*, trans. Denis Searby (Oxford: Oxford University Press, 2006), 77. An egregious example of a modern evasion of the dogma of biblical inerrancy may be found in the *New Jerusalem Biblical Commentary*, which argues that the truthfulness of the Bible consists not in its being free of error but in the fact that God manifests His faithfulness to His people through the Bible! *NJBC*, "Inspiration," Raymond Collins, para. 65.

7

Rule of Faith

SINCE THE HOLY SCRIPTURES ARE the written word of God, the affirmations that they make call for the assent of divine faith. It is true that not everything in the Scriptures is of equal importance:

> There are some things which we are to believe, about which we have faith for their own sake (*secundum se*), others, about which we have faith not for their own sake but only for the sake of other things. . . . The things which directly order us to eternal life belong of themselves (*per se*) to faith: for example the three Persons, the omnipotence of God, the mystery of the incarnation of Christ, and other such. . . . But some things are proposed in the Scriptures for our belief, not as being principally intended, but to manifest the former things, such as that Abraham had two sons, that a dead man rose again upon touching the bones of Eliseus, and such like things which are narrated in Sacred Scripture to manifest the divine majesty or the incarnation of Christ.[57]

[57] *Summa theol.* II-II, Q. 1, art. 6, ad 1. Billot expresses the same distinction when he writes that some things in the Bible are inspired "by direct intention," namely everything that produces speculative or affective knowledge of man's end and of the means thereto, while other things

Nevertheless, everything in the sacred writings is attested with the same authority, that of God revealing, and so St Thomas explains that the denial even of something which is proposed by the Scriptures not as being principally intended would nonetheless rank as heresy—"as for instance if someone said that Samuel was not the son of Elcana, for it follows that the divine Scripture would be false."[58]

The same author states that since everything affirmed by God through the biblical authors calls for the assent of faith on our part, Scripture can be called "a rule of faith," that is, something that governs what men must or must not believe:

> Since we have received the manifestation of God from sacred Scripture, we must preserve the things found in sacred Scripture as an excellent rule of faith (*quamdam optimam regulam veritatis*), neither increasing it by adding things to it, nor reducing it by removing things, nor corrupting it by expounding it ill.[59]

St Robert Bellarmine averred that Scripture was not given *properly and principally* as a rule of faith but rather as "a permanent reminder (*commonitorium*) to preserve and support the truth received from preaching," and that "by various proofs, examples,

---

are inspired by concomitance. Under the first heading he places "the whole economy of the Kingdom of Christ the Saviour, from its first preparation after the Fall of our first parents until its perfect constitution in the Church of the New Testament," while as examples of the latter he mentions Adam's age when he died and the fact that Paul left his cloak at Troas. Such details, he argues, are included so that the sacred history might be written "in a human and connatural way": *De Inspiratione*, 97–98.

58 *Summa theol.* I, Q. 32, art. 4.

59 *Commentary on the Divine Names*, ch. 2, lect. 1.

and exhortations, now instructing, now threatening, now consoling, it may help us in this pilgrimage." If it were given to be strictly speaking a rule of faith, he notes, then it would have to contain "all and only those things which of themselves pertain to the faith, as we see is done with a creed, which is truly called, and was composed so as to be, a brief rule of faith." Nevertheless, he allows that Scripture, though not principally written to be the rule of faith, is in fact a partial such rule: "The total rule of faith is the word of God, that is, the revelation of God made to the Church, and which is divided into two partial rules, Scripture and Tradition."[60]

Doubtless, as St Thomas remarks, "the truth of the faith is contained in sacred Scripture in a way that is spread out (*diffuse*), and in various styles, and in some places obscurely, so that much study and experience is needed to draw out the truth of the faith from sacred Scripture."[61] Nevertheless, whoever possesses the virtue of theological faith may by this virtue assent to whatever truths he reads and understands in the Bible, whether this understanding derives from his own study, or from another's teaching, or from a definition by the Church. In all these cases, he is assenting to God Himself.

[60] St Robert Bellarmine, *Controversiae*, "On the Word of God," Bk. IV, ch. 12. *Dei Verbum* 21 likewise affirms that the Bible and sacred tradition together form the supreme rule of faith.

[61] *Summa theol.* II-II, Q. 1, art. 9, ad 1.

8

Sufficiency of Holy Scripture

SINCE THE HOLY SCRIPTURES ARE, as St Augustine told the faithful in Hippo, a kind of letter sent from that City to which we are travelling as pilgrims, it is fitting that they contain in some manner all that we need for our journey thither.[62] But in what manner? Combining the approach of St Thomas with that of St Robert Bellarmine, we might distinguish three classes of truth contained in the word of God.

There are some truths in divine revelation that all Christians have always needed to know explicitly, and the Scriptures contain these things plainly. There are other truths contained in revelation that have not always and everywhere been necessary for all Christians to know explicitly, but which may have become so in the past or may become so in the future; these things are either plainly contained in Scripture, or else they may be deduced

[62] Likewise, St Cyril of Jerusalem: "Concerning the divine and holy mysteries of the faith, not even a casual statement must be delivered without the Holy Scriptures; nor must we be drawn aside by mere plausibility and artifices of speech. Even to me, who tell you these things, give not absolute credence, unless thou receive the proof of the things which I announce from the divine Scriptures. For this salvation which we believe depends not on ingenious reasoning, but on demonstration of the Holy Scriptures": *Catechetical Lectures*, IV.17; *PG* 33:476-77.

directly from what is contained in Scripture, rightly understood, without the use of non-scriptural premises. These two principles taken together may be called "the material sufficiency of Scripture." Finally, there are some revealed truths that pertain to those who have certain divinely instituted offices within the Church; these things are thus not necessarily contained in the Scriptures, since these latter are given to all. Yet these things too are contained in Scripture implicitly, in a more qualified sense of the word "implicitly," in that Scripture speaks to us of these divinely instituted offices and assures us that Christ will provide suitably for their exercise. Let us examine each category more closely.

1. Some things have always been necessary for *all* Christians to hold. No adult, outside imminent danger of death, is admitted to baptism if he is ignorant of these.[63] Therefore, just as God has made water easily available, since all are called to baptism, so He has placed the knowledge of these truths on the surface of the Scriptures. St Augustine thus affirms that "among the things that are plainly (*aperte*) laid down in Scripture are to be found all matters that sustain faith and the right manner of living (*mores vivendi*), that is, hope and love."[64] St Thomas, likewise, asserts: "Nothing necessary for faith is contained under the spiritual sense of Scripture which it does not plainly (*manifeste*) teach elsewhere by the literal sense."[65] St Robert Bellarmine, for his part, writes as follows:

63 Note that no adult may be baptized even in imminent danger of death if he is ignorant of the Trinity and the Incarnation: *Response of the Holy Office to the Bishop of Quebec*, January 25, 1703, DH 2380.

64 St Augustine, *De Doctrina Christiana*, II.14.

65 *Summa theol.* I, Q. 1, art. 10. He expresses himself more precisely here than in the *Quaestiones Quodlibetales* VII, Q. 6, art. 1, ad 3, where he had simply said that Scripture states nothing obscure which it does not

> Some parts of Christian doctrine, in matters of both faith and morals, are simply speaking necessary to all people for salvation: such are the knowledge of the articles of the Apostles' Creed, and also the knowledge of the ten commandments and of some sacraments. . . . I say that all those things were written down by the apostles which are necessary to all, and which they themselves had openly preached to all in common.[66]

Yet because every truth of faith surpasses man's mind, and because his capacity for perversity is great, even these truths may be brought into doubt or misunderstood by an ill-disposed or ignorant expositor of the Bible. Thus the Arians, though claiming to believe the Scriptures, did not accept that Jesus Christ is the Son of God in the manner taught by the Scriptures, and the Calvinists did not accept the doctrine of the descent of His soul into hell after death. Hence even in regard to this first class of truths, the sufficiency of the Scriptures does not exclude the necessity of the Church as teacher. There are many things, remarks Bellarmine, which are indeed taught by the Bible, but about which "if one were to strive only by testimonies of Scripture, the strife with the stubborn would never end."[67]

---

express plainly elsewhere. St Augustine, whom St Thomas is following here, remarked that "*almost* (*fere*) nothing is dug out of those obscure passages which may not be found set forth in the plainest language elsewhere": *De Doctrina Christiana*, II.8. Bellarmine observes that the meaning of most of the Apocalypse and of the beginning and the end of Ezekiel is not explained elsewhere: *Controversiae*, "On the Word of God," Bk. III, ch. 2.

66 St Robert Bellarmine, *Controversiae*, "On the Word of God," Bk. IV, ch. 11.

67 Ibid., ch. 4.

2. There are other truths contained in divine revelation which the Church has not always and everywhere insisted that all Christians must explicitly profess:

> Other things are not so necessary that a man could not be saved without the explicit knowledge and faith and profession of them, provided he have a ready will to accept and believe them when they shall have been duly proposed to him by the Church.[68]

Such truths may, though need not, be affirmed explicitly by Scripture, although the principle of the "material sufficiency of Scripture" means that if they are not explicitly affirmed, they can be deduced from it, rightly understood, without the aid of non-scriptural premises.[69] Truths of this kind might include the Assumption of the Blessed Virgin Mary and the primacy of the church of Rome.[70] Thus, the Assumption is not plainly taught by Scripture, but one could hold that it follows, for example, from Psalm 112:4 and 1 Corinthians 11:7, or Psalm 131:8 and Luke 1:35 rightly understood.[71]

---

[68] Ibid., ch. 11. It may however become necessary that a Christian obtain explicit knowledge of these truths, especially if he is living in a time and place when they are attacked.

[69] *De Veritate*, Q. 14, art. 10, ad 11: "We do not believe in the successors of the apostles and prophets except insofar as these announce to us the thing which those men left in their writings." Cf. St John Henry Newman, *Development of Christian Doctrine*, Ch. 7, 4, 4: "Nor am I aware that later Post-tridentine writers deny that the whole Catholic faith may be proved from Scripture, though they would certainly maintain that it is not to be found on the surface of it, nor in such sense that it may be gained from Scripture without the aid of Tradition."

[70] For *Romanitas* as a note of the Church, see Alan Fimister, *The Iron Scepter of the Son of Man* (Lincoln, NE: Os Justi Press, forthcoming).

[71] Ps. 112:4: "The Lord is high above all nations and his glory above the heavens"; 1 Cor. 11:7: "The woman is the glory of the man"; Ps. 131:8:

3. Finally, there are certain revealed truths, which have always been necessary for the spiritual rulers and ministers of the Church to know, but which are not necessarily contained in the Scriptures. St Thomas writes:

> Sacred Scripture is put forward to all in general; thus the form of baptism, which can be administered by all, had to be expressed in Sacred Scripture, and likewise the form of the Eucharist, which expresses the faith in that sacrament, a faith necessary for salvation. But the form of the other sacraments is not found to have been placed into Scripture, but rather the Church has them from the tradition of the apostles, who received them from the Lord.[72]

Bellarmine, similarly, affirms that the apostles preached some things which are necessary "only for prelates, bishops, and priests," such as "the manner of governing the Church, of administering the sacraments and of responding to heretics," and that these were not all placed in the Scriptures.[73] Another example of a divinely revealed truth necessary for the clergy to know, but not set forth in Scripture or strictly deducible from it, may be the validity of baptism when conferred by non-Catholics.[74]

"Arise, O Lord, into thy resting-place, thou and the ark, which thou hast sanctified"; Lk. 1:35: "The Holy Ghost shall come upon thee, and the power of the most High shall overshadow thee."

72 *Scriptum super Sententiis*, IV, dist. 23, Q. 1, art. 4, qa. 1, ad 1. He gives the same teaching in *Summa theol.* III, Q. 64, art. 2, ad 1, where those essential elements of the sacraments not mentioned in Scripture are said to have come to the Church *ex familiari apostolorum traditione* ("from the household customs passed on from the apostles").

73 *Controversiae*, "On the Word of God," Bk. IV, ch. 11.

74 Speaking about the Church's practice of not rebaptizing heretics, St Augustine writes: "The custom, which is opposed to Cyprian, may be

The doctrine of the material sufficiency of Scripture, thus understood in this manner, may claim impressive testimonies:[75] it has not however been defined by the Church. The Council of Trent limited itself to teaching that the gospel, "the font of all saving truth and discipline of morals," has come to us from Christ through the apostles, by means both of their writings and of the unwritten traditions (*in libris scriptis et sine scripto traditionibus*) which they left to the Church.[76] The Second Vatican Council, for its part, cautiously stated: "It is not from Sacred Scripture alone that the Church draws her certainty about everything which has been revealed,"[77] a statement leaving it undetermined whether other sources have increased her certainty in scope or in intensity.

This material sufficiency of Scripture must be carefully distinguished from the assertion of the "formal sufficiency" of Scripture, an assertion commonly summarized by the phrase *sola Scriptura* ("by Scripture alone"). This latter doctrine holds that human beings may gain an understanding of the word of God sufficient for their salvation simply by reading a copy of the Bible in any

---

supposed to have had its origin in apostolic tradition, just as there are many things which are observed by the whole Church, and therefore are fairly held to have been enjoined (*praecepta*) by the apostles, which yet are not mentioned in their writings": *On Baptism against the Donatists*, IV.23. The examples given by St Basil of unwritten traditions received from the apostles relate to the correct conduct of the liturgy by the sacred ministers: *On the Holy Spirit*, ch. 27.66.

[75] For further references, other than those found in the present work, see Congar, *Tradition and Traditions*, 107–18.

[76] Session IV, *Decree on the Reception of the Sacred Books and Traditions*, DH 1501. An earlier draft of this decree, stating that the gospel was contained partly in Scripture and partly in tradition, was revised, perhaps at the request of Angelo Bonucci, the General of the Servite Order. See Congar, *Tradition and Traditions*, 164–65.

[77] *Dei Verbum* 9.

language. Such a position, as well as raising insuperable problems about determining the contents of the canon and the reliability of a given translation,[78] also contradicts itself in that Scripture itself does not teach this doctrine but rather by clear implication rejects it:

> Behold a man of Ethiopia, an eunuch, of great authority under Candace the queen of the Ethiopians, who had charge over all her treasures, had come to Jerusalem to adore. And he was returning, sitting in his chariot, and reading Isaias the prophet. And the Spirit said to Philip: Go near, and join thyself to this chariot. And Philip running thither, heard him reading the prophet Isaias. And he said: Thinkest thou that thou understandest what thou readest? Who said: And how can I, unless some man shew me? And he desired Philip that he would come up and sit with him.[79]

[78] See Section 12, "The Canon," and Section 13, "The Septuagint and the Vulgate." Some Protestant writers have described the Bible as "a fallible collection of infallible books." Evidently, this is equivalent to saying: "I think the Bible is infallible (i.e., inerrant), but I could be wrong."

[79] See Acts 8:27–31.

9

Interpretation of Scripture

WITH HIS CHARACTERISTIC SUPERNATURAL SARCASM, St Jerome observed: "The art of interpreting the scriptures is the only one of which all men everywhere claim to be masters."[80] St Robert Bellarmine explains that the Scriptures are difficult to understand both because of what they describe and because of their manner of speaking.[81] They speak of the highest truths: the divine Trinity, the incarnation of the Word, the heavenly sacraments, the nature of the angels, the workings of God in human souls, eternal predestination and reprobation. Among their obscurities of manner, Bellarmine notes that a great part of the Bible consists in poetical predictions, "than which there is nothing harder or more obscure," and that it contains apparent (though not real) contradictions, ambiguous phrases, sentences without a main verb, anticipations of what will be explained only later, Hebraisms, and figures of speech of many kinds.

St Augustine, to be sure, in a letter to a fellow Catholic, wrote: "It is not that there is a great difficulty in coming through them [the Scriptures] to know the things necessary to salvation."[82] We

[80] Letter 53.7, *To Paulinus*.

[81] *Controversiae*, "On the Word of God," Bk. III.1.

[82] Letter 137.3, *To Volusianus*.

should, however, understand this with the qualification "provided that the reader has the virtue of faith and has not put himself under the tutelage of heretical teachers," since the bishop of Hippo was aware that the Donatists, the Arians, and the Pelagians read the same Bible as he. He was also aware, like Bellarmine, that even the orthodox believer may find the Scriptures in places hard or impossible to understand, and he suggested why the Holy Spirit had inspired writings of such a kind:

> Hasty and careless readers are led astray by many and manifold obscurities and ambiguities, substituting one meaning for another; and in some places they cannot hit upon even a fair interpretation. Some of the expressions are so obscure as to shroud the meaning in the thickest darkness. And I do not doubt that all this was divinely arranged for the purpose of subduing pride by toil, and of preventing a feeling of satiety in the intellect, which generally holds in small esteem what is discovered without difficulty.[83]

St Vincent of Lérins, in the fifth century, provides the classic expression of the Catholic position according to which the perfection of Scripture does not obviate but rather postulates an authorized interpreter:

> We must, the Lord helping, fortify our own belief in two ways; first, by the authority of the divine Law, and then, by

[83] *De Doctrina Christiana*, II.7. Tertullian, for his part, went so far as to affirm: "Nor do I risk contradiction in saying that the very Scriptures were even arranged by the will of God in such a manner as to furnish materials for heretics, inasmuch as I read that 'there must be heresies,' which there cannot be without the Scriptures": *On the Prescriptions against Heretics*, 39.

> the tradition of the Catholic Church. But here some one perhaps will ask: "Since the canon of Scripture is complete (*perfectus*), and sufficient of itself for everything, and more than sufficient (*sibique ad omnia satis superque sufficiat*), what need is there to join with it the authority of the Church's interpretation?" For this reason — because, owing to the depth of Holy Scripture, all do not accept it in one and the same sense, but one understands its words in one way, another in another; so that it seems to be capable of as many interpretations as there are interpreters.[84]

The Council of Trent therefore declared that it pertains to the Church "to judge the true meaning and interpretation of the sacred Scriptures," and forbade anyone "in matters of faith and morals, pertaining to the building up of Christian doctrine, twisting sacred Scripture to his own judgements, to interpret it contrary to that sense which the Church has held and does hold."[85] The Church's task of interpretation may be exercised negatively when accredited teachers explain that a certain passage cannot have the meaning which some people claim for it—when this meaning is contrary to the faith of the Church.[86] It is exercised positively, when she specifies the meaning that a given passage

---

[84] *Commonitorium*, ch. 2. For an extended discussion, see Casey Chalk, *The Obscurity of Scripture: Disputing* Sola Scriptura *and the Protestant Notion of Biblical Perspicuity* (Steubenville, OH: Emmaus Road, 2023).

[85] Session IV, *Decree on the Vulgate Edition of the Books and of the Manner of Interpreting Sacred Scripture*. Cf. *Dei Verbum* 12.

[86] For example, even without specifying the meaning of Prov. 8:22, "The Lord brought me forth at the beginning of his works," the Catholic teacher could explain that it did not have the sense which Arius attributed to it.

must be understood to bear.[87] Pope St Pius X formally condemned the proposition that "even by dogmatic definitions the Church's magisterium cannot determine the genuine sense of the Sacred Scriptures."[88] As with her other teachings, the Church's scriptural interpretations need not take the form of a solemn definition, but may be manifested in other ways, such as constant liturgical practice.[89]

The same council forbade anyone to interpret Scripture "against the unanimous consent of the Fathers, even if such interpretations should never be made public."[90] Hence, for example, it would be illegitimate, even if one held to the orthodox position on the Eucharist, to interpret "eating Christ's flesh" in chapter

---

[87] For example, canon 12 of the Second Council of Constantinople declares that the words of the apostle Thomas "My Lord and My God" were a confession of the divinity of Christ, and anathematizes those who claim that they were an expression of simple thanksgiving to God for the resurrection.

[88] *Lamentabili Sane* 4.

[89] For example, the reference to the sacrifice of Abel in the Roman Canon of the Mass would seem to be incompatible with the claim that the story of Cain and Abel in Genesis is fiction. How would it be compatible with the dignity of the Eucharistic sacrifice to ask God to accept it as He "accepted" a fictional offering?

[90] Session IV. Billot observes that the rule established by the Tridentine decree applies not only to the interpretation of individual passages, but also to general principles of interpretation which are universally received within the Church, for example, that "Scripture is accustomed to refer to the ultimate and universal judgement whatever pertains to the rewards and punishments of the future life, and to make those people whom the consummation of the age will find alive to stand for all men in general, whatever time they may have lived or may live or may be going to live"; *De Inspiratione*, 168–69. Biblical exhortations to prepare for the second coming of Christ are therefore also exhortations to prepare for death.

six of St John's gospel to be simply a reference to faith in Him. This prohibition is necessary not only because of the presumption implied in supposing oneself wiser than those saints, but also and especially because such unanimous consent is a strong sign of the apostolicity of the interpretation in question. The First Vatican Council therefore corrected an unduly minimizing interpretation of the Tridentine decree, and explained that this decree not only forbids one to declare something to be false which the Church, or the unanimity of the Fathers, judges to be asserted by a passage of Scripture pertaining to faith or morals, but that it also obliges Catholics to hold this to be the correct interpretation of the passage in question.[91] Likewise, the second proposition condemned in *Lamentabili Sane* is: "The Church's interpretation of the sacred books is by no means to be rejected; nevertheless, it is subject to the more accurate judgment and correction of the exegetes."

Again, it would be too niggardly an interpretation of the Tridentine decree to suppose that it referred only to those passages of Scripture that affirm something revealed for its own

[91] *Dei Filius*, ch. 2: "Now since the decree on the interpretation of Holy Scripture, profitably made by the Council of Trent, with the intention of constraining rash speculation, has been wrongly interpreted by some, we renew that decree and declare its meaning to be as follows: that in matters of faith and morals, belonging as they do to the establishing of Christian doctrine, that meaning of Holy Scripture must be held to be the true one, which Holy Mother Church held and holds, since it is her right to judge of the true meaning and interpretation of Holy Scripture." The *Adnotationes* to the first schema of *Dei Filius* show that this clarification was made to rebut those claiming it to be sufficient for exegetes not to contradict the dogmas taught by the Fathers: *Acta et decreta sacrosancti oecumenici concilii Vaticani* (Fribourg: Herder, 1892), Coll. Lacensis, VII, 523.

sake and thus capable of being placed in a creed. The virtuous acts performed by the scriptural saints and the miraculous acts performed by God in the Old Testament also "pertain to the building up of Christian doctrine."[92] Hence, it would be wrong, for example, to argue in company with many modern exegetes that Job was a rebel against God and doubted divine justice, when the Fathers unanimously speak of him as a hero of faith.[93]

In 1902, Pope Leo XIII established the Pontifical Biblical Commission by his apostolic letter *Vigilantiae*.[94] Its mandate was confirmed in 1907 by Pope Pius X in *Praestantia Scripturae Sacrae*. The latter pope declared that its decisions were to be received with the same assent as the doctrinal declarations of the Holy Office.[95] During several pontificates, the Commission promulgated decrees about the authorship and interpretation of Scripture; it is not true, as is often stated or assumed, that these decrees were later

[92] Council of Trent, Session IV.

[93] For a brief account of this contrast, see Fr Thomas Crean, O.P., "Ancients and Moderns on the Patience of Job," http://christendom-awake.org/pages/thomas-crean/job.htm.

[94] *Enchiridion Biblicum*, 4th ed. (Rome, 1961), 64–68.

[95] "We find it necessary to declare and prescribe, as We do now declare and expressly prescribe, that all are bound in conscience to submit to the decisions of the Biblical Commission, which have been given in the past and which shall be given in the future, in the same way as to the Decrees which appertain to doctrine, issued by the Sacred Congregations and approved by the Sovereign Pontiff. Nor can they escape the stigma both of disobedience and of temerity nor be free from grave guilt as often as they impugn these decisions either in word or writing; and this, over and above the scandal which they give and the sins of which they may be the cause before God by making other statements on these matters which are very frequently both rash and false"; DH 3503.

annulled.[96] Pope Paul VI removed all magisterial authority from the Pontifical Biblical Commission, reconstituting it as a simple committee of scholars whose expertise is valued by the Holy See.[97] Since then, its assertions have no claim on the religious assent of Catholics, although they may elicit a simply human assent, in proportion to the scholarship and piety of their authors, and the strength of the arguments that they offer.

Although the Church must always have sufficient understanding of the Scriptures to accomplish the tasks necessary for the salvation of souls, it does not follow that an understanding of every part of Scripture, for example of every prophecy in the Apocalypse of St John, is always found within the episcopate.[98] Even after the end of the apostolic age, the Holy Spirit can enlighten any of the faithful about the meaning, or some part of the meaning, of a given passage of Scripture. St Thomas explains that the gift of understanding, possessed by all those in a state of grace, strengthens the mind to reach meanings that lie beneath the inspired words.[99] We may even say that God reveals things

96 See Fr Sean Kopczynski, "Rediscovering the Decrees of the Pontifical Biblical Commission," *Living Tradition* 94 (2001), www.rtforum.org/lt/lt94.html.

97 "The Pontifical Biblical Commission, in its new form after the Second Vatican Council, is not an organ of the teaching office, but rather a commission of scholars": Joseph Ratzinger, preface to *The Interpretation of the Bible in the Church* (Rome: Pontifical Biblical Commission, 1993).

98 Bellarmine observes: "God . . . has not made everything which is contained in Scripture to be an article of faith which His Church must know, since there are many passages which are very doubtful and obscure, and which will probably remain so, as long as the world shall last": *Vindiciae, de Verbo Dei*, bk. 2, ad caput 7.

99 *Summa theol.* II-II, Q. 8, art. 1. In modern times, many prestigious biblical commentaries are written by men without faith. While containing some useful things, they present spiritual danger to those who are

in this way, using the word "revelation" in its broader sense.[100] Hence, there is room for the understanding of Scripture to grow within the Church, even though public revelation finished with the apostles. "Thou, O Daniel, shut up the words, and seal the book, even to the time appointed: many shall pass over, and knowledge shall be manifold."[101]

---

insufficiently prepared, and it would be an aberration to make them one's principal guides to the meaning of Scripture. "There is indeed nothing more full of rashness . . . than in the case of each several book, to desert expounders who profess that they hold them and that they can deliver them to their scholars, and to seek their meaning from those who, I know not from what cause compelling, have proclaimed a most bitter war against the framers and authors of them. For—to speak of systems of teaching wherein a reader may err without sacrilege—who ever thought that the hidden and dark books of Aristotle should be expounded to him by someone who was Aristotle's enemy?": St Augustine, *On the Profit of Believing* 13.

[100] For examples of the word *revelatio* and its cognates being applied to God's enlightenment of the Church, and of individual believers, even after the apostolic age, see Congar, *Tradition and Traditions*, 92 and 119–25.

[101] Dan. 12:4. *Dei Verbum* 8 states: "There is a growth in the understanding of the realities and the words which have been handed down. This happens through the contemplation and study made by believers, who treasure these things in their hearts, through a penetrating understanding of the spiritual realities which they experience, and through the preaching of those who have received through episcopal succession the sure gift of truth." John Lamont has proposed that the principle that public revelation ended with the death of the apostles should be understood as stating not that all propositions that will be taught by the Church as divinely revealed were already taught by the apostles (or are conclusions from two premises taught by them) but that "no new salvific realities have been revealed by God to mankind." In practice, this opinion seems to converge with our view that the Holy Spirit continues to enlighten the Church about the meaning of the propositions taught in Scripture. See Lamont, *Divine Faith*, 179.

10

The Plurality of Senses

THE EXISTENCE IN SCRIPTURE of a sense deeper than that which appears on the surface is itself taught by Scripture. The writers of the Old Testament do not explicitly assert this; to prevent erroneous and fantastical interpretations, it was fitting that the existence of this deeper sense not be made known to all until the coming of Christ, in whose light alone it may be safely sought. Yet even in the Old Testament, the fact of a spiritual sense was obscurely taught. In the book received by the prophet Ezekiel, written both on the inside and on the outside, St Jerome sees a type of Scripture with its twofold meaning.[102] St Gregory the Great, commenting on the same passage, explains: "The book of sacred eloquence is written inwardly through allegory, outwardly through the history."[103] The same pope compared the faithful student of Scripture to Jacob's sheep, before whom were set both the peeled and the unpeeled bark.[104]

The New Testament teaches the existence of the spiritual sense of Scripture explicitly. St Paul, commenting on the history of

---

[102] *Commentary on Ezekiel*, ch. 2.

[103] *Homilies on Ezekiel*, I.9.29-30. See also St Gregory Nazianzen, *Carmina* II.7: "There is also with us a twofold sense of divine Scripture, one inward and spiritual, the other outward."

[104] *Moralia* 21.2, referring to Gen. 30:37–39.

Sarah and Hagar, observes: "These things are said by an allegory (ἀλληγορούμενα)."[105] Elsewhere, having described the vicissitudes of the chosen people in the wilderness, he concludes: "All these things happened to them in figure (τυπικῶς): and they are written for our correction."[106] In the Epistle to the Hebrews, he explains that the tabernacle of the Law of Moses was so arranged by the Holy Spirit that it would be a symbol (παραβολή) of sacred history.[107] The elevation of the brazen serpent is presented in St John's gospel as a prefigurement of the crucifixion.[108] St Peter describes baptism as an "antitype" (ἀντίτυπον) of the salvation which Noah's ark brought through the waters of the flood—that is, a realization of the prefigurement given by Noah.[109] Following the example of the apostles, and of Christ Himself, the Fathers of the Church delighted in uncovering the types of the Old Testament. St Augustine's aphorism is well known: *In veteri [testamento] novum latet, et in novo vetus patet.*[110]

St Thomas explains the basis of the spiritual sense thus: "The author of Sacred Scripture is God, in whose power it is to signify His meaning not only by words, as men also can do, but also by things themselves." Accordingly, whereas the literal sense of Scripture is that which its human and divine authors intended to express by its words, its spiritual sense is that which God

105 Gal. 4:24.

106 1 Cor. 10:11.

107 Heb. 9:9.

108 John 3:14.

109 1 Pet. 3:21. In this word, "anti" means "over against," as in a matching pair.

110 "The New Testament lies hidden in the Old, and the Old is made clear in the New"; cf. *Questions on the Heptateuch*, II.73. The expression is quoted in *Dei Verbum* 16.

alone intended to express by the events which those words record. Defending the Old Testament against one of the principal Manichees of his day, St Augustine writes of the Jews: "Not only the speech of these men, but their life also was prophetic; and the whole kingdom of the Hebrews was like a great prophet."[111]

There is thus an analogy between the written word of God and the Christian sacraments.[112] The sacraments are external rites which signify some reality, called the *res et sacramentum*, which itself signifies an ultimate reality: thus, the consecration of bread and wine signifies and effects the natural body of Christ on the altar, which in turn signifies His Mystical Body. In a similar way, a passage of Scripture, for example a narration in the Old Testament, signifies certain past events which themselves signify future ones.

Within the spiritual sense itself, it is customary to distinguish three species: the allegorical, the anagogical, and the moral.[113] Hence, adding the literal sense, one reaches "the four senses of Scripture." St Thomas's most extensive account of the relation between them comes in his *Quaestiones Quodlibetales*:

> Sacred Scripture manifests in two ways the truth which it contains: by words and by the figures of things. The manifestation which takes place through words produces the historic or literal sense, and so everything which is rightly

[111] *Against Faustus*, XX.24.

[112] Billot, *De Inspiratione*, 88.

[113] The terminology used by the Fathers fluctuates, as Bellarmine remarks: *Controversiae*, "On the Word of God," Bk. III, ch. 3. For example, they sometimes used "allegorical" for any spiritual sense. The moral sense is also known as the tropological sense. Modern writers often refer to the allegorical sense as "typology."

understood from the meaning of the words themselves pertains to the literal sense. But the spiritual sense, as has been said, consists in the fact that some things are expressed by the figure of other things, since visible things are usually figures of invisible ones, as Dionysus says. Hence, this sense which is drawn from figures is called spiritual.

Now, the truth which Sacred Scripture conveys by the figures of things has two purposes, namely right belief and right action. When it is for right action, it is a moral sense, also called tropological. When it is for right belief, a distinction must be drawn in accordance with the order of things to be believed. For, as Dionysius says in chapter four of *The Heavenly Hierarchy*, the position of the Church is a middle one between that of the synagogue and that of the Church triumphant. Therefore, the old Testament was a figure of the new, while the old and the new together are a figure of heavenly things.

Therefore, the spiritual sense which is ordered to right belief can be based in that kind of representation by which the old Testament prefigures the new, in which case it is an allegorical or typical sense, and in this case, things which happened in the old Testament are expounded of Christ and of the Church; or else, it can be based in that kind of representation by which the new and the old together signify the Church triumphant, and in that case it is an anagogical sense.[114]

For example, Solomon in building his temple is, by allegory, a type of Christ establishing His earthly Church, and by anagogy,

[114] *Quaestiones Quodlibetales* VII, Q. 6, art. 2.

a type of Christ establishing His heavenly one, while by the moral sense, he represents any believer who prepares his soul to be a dwelling-place for God. Pushing his analysis further, the Common Doctor continues:

> These four senses are not attributed to Sacred Scripture as if each part of it should be expounded according to all four: sometimes it is to be expounded with all four, sometimes with three, sometimes with two, and sometimes with only one. For in sacred Scripture, later things are mostly signified by earlier ones, and so sometimes in sacred Scripture, something is said according to the literal sense about an earlier thing which can be spiritually interpreted about a later thing, but not *vice versa.*
>
> Now among all the things which are related in Sacred Scripture, the first are the things which belong to the Old Testament, and so what belongs according to the literal sense to the deeds of the Old Testament can be expounded in four senses. Second come the things which pertain to the Church in this present age. Among these, the things which pertain to the Head are earlier than those which pertain to the members, for the true body of Christ, and the things which were done in it, are figures of the mystical body of Christ and of the things which are done in the Mystical Body, so that in Him, Christ, we may draw our model for living. In Christ, also, future glory is shown to us in advance. Therefore, the things which are said literally of Christ the Head may be interpreted allegorically, in reference to His Mystical Body; and morally, in reference to our actions, which must be reformed according to Him; and anagogically, insofar as in Christ we have the path to glory.

For example, by feeding the five thousand, Christ symbolized how, as head of the earthly Church and through her action, He would feed the faithful on earth with the Holy Eucharist, and how, as simultaneously head of the Church triumphant, He would lead them through this sacrament to the heavenly union which it signifies.[115] According to the moral sense, the feeding symbolizes the acts by which any Christian, such as a priest or parent, supernaturally feeds those under his care.

> But when according to the letter, something is said about the Church, it cannot be interpreted allegorically, unless perhaps things said of the primitive Church should be expounded of some later state of the Church in this present age; yet they can be interpreted both morally and anagogically.

Thus, when the Church on earth prayed for Peter in prison (Acts 12:5), she was an image both of the individual soul praying for pastors to be released from material or moral chains, and of the heavenly Church praying for the same end. He continues:

> Those things which are said about morals according to the literal sense are not generally expounded except allegorically.

For example, Rabanus Maurus interprets the praise of the worthy wife in Ecclesiasticus 26 as an encomium to the Church.[116] Finally, St Thomas notes:

---

[115] Ibid., ad 4: "Just as the allegorical sense pertains to Christ, inasmuch as He is the head of the militant Church, justifying her and infusing grace into her, so also the anagogical sense pertains to Him inasmuch as He is the head of the triumphant Church, and glorifies her."

[116] Commenting on the words "As golden pillars upon bases of silver, so are the firm feet upon the soles of a steady woman," Rabanus Maurus

> Those things which according to the literal sense pertain to the state of glory are not generally expounded in any other sense, since they are not figures of other things, but are prefigured by everything else.[117]

Thus, the descriptions of the heavenly city in the Apocalypse are expounded only "literally," that is, as referring only to the heavenly city and not to anything beyond it.

Since God alone can so guide the course of events, willing or permitting the actions of free agents in such a way that history symbolizes what He will do in the Church or the soul, no historical record except for one composed by divine inspiration can bear a spiritual sense.[118] Since one thing can resemble many—a lion, for example, may be a symbol both of Christ on account of its strength, and of the devil on account of its ferocity—the spiritual sense, though certain in itself, has by itself less power to produce conviction than the literal. Therefore, theological arguments are not generally based on it alone.[119] Bellarmine, however, adds that

---

writes: "The golden columns are the holy doctors, who are placed on silver bases when they rest their preaching on the words of Sacred Scripture. Their feet are firmly established upon the soles of a steady woman, since their preaching, by which they sowed the word of God throughout the world, advances while resting firmly upon the stability of the Catholic faith."

[117] *Quaestiones Quodlibetales* VII, Q. 6, art. 2.

[118] Ibid., art. 3. Cf. St Gregory, *Moralia*, XX.1: "To say nothing of the weightiness of its subjects, Sacred Scripture surpasses all forms of knowledge and teaching even by the manner of its speech, since in one and the same word, while it unfolds its narration, it brings forth a mystery, and has the art so to tell the past that merely by that alone it may announce the future."

[119] *Summa theol.* I, Q. 1, art. 10, ad 1. Cf. St Augustine, Letter 93.24, *To Vincentius the Donatist*: "How would it not be great impudence for

if it is clear "from Scripture, from the tradition of the Church, or from the common teaching of the holy Fathers" that a given passage has a given mystical sense, one can argue from that as efficaciously as from the literal.[120]

Since the "literal sense" is that which the author intends by the words, and since God is the primary author of Scripture, one may also attribute several literal senses to a given passage. For example, the phrase "in the beginning"—as found in the sentence "In the beginning God created heaven and earth"—may be understood to mean both "at the beginning of time" and "in the Word," as the beginning or principle of creatures. Since both interpretations yield a true sense which was seen to be true by God, and since God cannot fail to love any truth, both senses may be called the literal meaning of the words.[121] This kind of plurality of literal senses, writes the Angelic Doctor, pertains to the dignity of divine Scripture, "so that each man marvels to find his thoughts expressed in the words of Holy Writ." It is quite possible, he continues, that God enlightened the human authors themselves to understand in this way several meanings in their

someone to try to interpret something allegorically in his own favor, unless he also has clear passages (*manifesta testimonia*) in the light of which the obscure ones may be illumined?"

[120] *Vindiciae, de Verbo Dei*, bk. III, ad cap. 3.

[121] *Summa theol.* I, Q. 10, art. 1, where St Thomas appeals to St Augustine's discussion of this verse in *Confessions*, Bk. XII. In his discussion of 1 Pet. 3:18–21, St Augustine again allows the possibility of a plurality of literal senses: Letter 164.22. Bellarmine defends the same opinion, and gives the example of the verse in Psalm 109, "thou art my son, this day have I begotten you," which is interpreted to signify Christ's resurrection in Acts 13:33, His divinity in Heb. 1:5, and His high priesthood in Heb. 5:5; *Vindiciae, de Verbo Dei*, Bk. III, ad cap. 3.

own words. However, this is not necessary for the concept of a plurality of literal senses:

> Even if certain truths are applied (*aptentur*) by commentators to sacred Scripture that were not understood by the author, without doubt the Holy Spirit understood them, since he is the principal author of divine Scripture. Consequently every truth that can be applied to the sacred text without prejudice to the context (*salva litterae circumstantia*) is a sense of Holy Scripture.[122]

Normally, however, when we speak of the literal sense, we mean that which the human author also intended.

Modern authors have discussed the presence in Scripture of a *sensus plenior* ("fuller sense").[123] Correctly understood, this appears to be simply what St Thomas is describing here.[124] Less acceptable would be the suggestion that a *sensus plenior* involves the scriptural authors not understanding what they *themselves* meant: "it is unsatisfactory to see part of the Scriptural message which Christians are supposed to believe as springing from ignorance or error."[125]

---

122 *De Potentia*, Q. 4, art. 1.

123 The phrase appears to have been coined by Andrés Fernàndez in 1927. See Matthew Dunn, "Raymond Brown and the *sensus plenior* interpretation of the Bible," *Studies in Religion* 36 (3–4): 531–51.

124 It should not, however, be used to deny that the Old Testament prophets had true foreknowledge of the Christian dispensation.

125 Lamont, *Divine Faith*, 156. The modern *Catechism of the Catholic Church* speaks of the literal and the threefold spiritual sense of Scripture, but not of the *sensus plenior.*

11

Literary Genres

SINCE "IN SCRIPTURE, DIVINE THINGS are conveyed to us in the manner which men are accustomed to employ,"[126] the inspired books display a variety of literary forms, as is obvious.[127] Speaking somewhat hyperbolically, Pope Pius XII affirmed that "as the substantial Word of God became like to men in all things except sin, so the words of God, expressed in human language, are made like to human speech in every respect, except error." Qualifying his own words, he observed that of the modes of expression (*rationes loquendi*) found among ancient Oriental peoples, "none is excluded from the sacred books, provided the way of speaking adopted is in no way inconsistent with the holiness and truth of God."[128] It is thus insufficient that a given "literary genre" express the truth; it must be itself suited to the divine things which it conveys. To take an extreme example, it would be contrary to the dignity of Scripture to express the doctrine of human justification by means of limericks.

No support can be found among the Fathers or Doctors of the Church for the opinion that the inspired writers sometimes

[126] St Thomas Aquinas, *Commentary on the Epistle to the Hebrews*, ch. 1, lect. 1.

[127] Cf. *Dei Verbum* 12.

[128] *Divino Afflante Spiritu* 37.

composed fictional stories in order to express their doctrine, whether such alleged works be placed in the literary genre of myth[129] or in that of "historical fiction."[130] On the contrary, these saints often warn that the existence in Scripture of a spiritual sense must not be made into a pretext for overlooking or denying the historical events which the Bible relates. Thus St Jerome finds fault with Origen's exegesis of the book of Genesis: "He so allegorizes Paradise as to destroy historical truth, understanding angels instead of trees, heavenly virtues instead of rivers, and he overthrows all that is contained in the history of Paradise by his figurative interpretation."[131] St Thomas Aquinas remarks that the things that Scripture tells us about the garden of Eden are related "in the manner of a historical narrative" (rather than, say, in the manner of a parable or a vision), and should be understood accordingly.[132]

St Gregory the Great, commenting on the spiritual senses of the Book of Job, often exhorts the reader in such terms as these: "This we most earnestly entreat, that he who lifts up his mind to the spiritual signification should not desist from his reverence for the history (*a veneratione historiae*)."[133] When replying to the

[129] Billot's definition of myth is useful: "A traditional fable which is taken by the masses to be a true history, which expresses in a highly imaginative way either some religious dogma, or some law of nature, or some primeval event": *De Inspiratione*, 146.

[130] That is, a form of fiction which is given the appearance of history by the mention of real historical persons either as the characters in the story or as contemporaneous with its characters, and where the events related are such as could without incongruity have occurred during the period when these historical persons lived.

[131] *Letter to Pammachius on Origen*, 7.

[132] *Summa theol.* I, Q. 102, art. 2.

[133] *Moralia* I.56. An alternative reading in the manuscripts is *a vera ratione historiae*, from the true meaning of the history.

Emperor Julian's mocking enquiry about the language in which the serpent spoke to Eve, St Cyril of Alexandria asserted uncompromisingly that "there is nothing at all legendary (μυθικόν) in them," that is, in the Scriptures.[134] In the prologue to his *Commentary on the Book of Job*, St Thomas considered the opinion of "some people" that the Book of Job might be a work of fiction (*quaedam parabola*): he rejected this opinion as incompatible with the allusions made to Job elsewhere in the Bible, for example with St James's exhortation to imitation Job's patience (Jas. 5:11).[135] Presumably St Thomas thought it unworthy of an apostle to hold up a merely fictional character as a model for the faithful.

The Pontifical Biblical Commission in 1905 laid down the general principle that the sacred authors are not to be supposed to have communicated their doctrine by means of historical fiction. While not excluding the possibility that there could be instances of such a literary genre within the Bible, the commission stated that it would be necessary for solid proofs to be given before a Catholic could assert that the genre had in fact been used, a thing "not to be easily or rashly admitted."[136] Speaking of the first

[134] *PG* 76:635.

[135] Aquinas may have had in mind the twelfth-century Jewish philosopher Maimonides, who had treated the book as fictional. St Robert Bellarmine qualifies the opinion that the book of Job is fictional, which he attributes to Martin Luther and to certain rabbis, as heretical: *Controversiae*, "On the Word of God," Bk. I, ch. 5.

[136] DH 3373. This magisterial intervention also largely put an end to the suggestion that the historical books of the Bible were true only "according to the appearances"—i.e., that in saying that something had happened, they only meant to affirm that people in general said that it had happened. This theory had been briefly popular around the turn of the twentieth century. See *DTC*, "Inspiration de l'Écriture," V. Effet principal: l'inerrance. Benedict XV alluded to the same theory in

eleven chapters of the Book of Genesis, Pope Pius XII taught that they belong to the category of history (*ad genus historiae*), not of myth.[137] The second Vatican Council unequivocally rejected the claim that any part of the four gospels was fictitious:

> Holy Mother Church has firmly and with absolute constancy held, and continues to hold, that the four Gospels just named, whose historical character the Church unhesitatingly asserts, faithfully hand on what Jesus Christ, while living among men, really did and taught for their eternal salvation until the day He was taken up into heaven.[138]

Finally, we may note that it is the custom of the Church to honor all those whose sanctity is portrayed in the Old Testament, including persons mentioned in books which some exegetes have claimed for the genre of historical fiction.[139]

Spiritus Paraclitus 22: "Those . . . who hold that the historical portions of Scripture do not rest on the absolute truth of the facts but merely upon what they are pleased to term their relative truth, namely, what people then commonly thought . . . dissent from the Church's teaching."

137 *Humani Generis* 38–39.

138 *Dei Verbum* 19.

139 For example, the archangel Raphael, who is mentioned only in the Book of Tobit, and Esther and Judith, whose examples are celebrated along with those of Sara and Rebecca by the *Pontificale Romanum* in the rite of blessing and coronation of a queen. Similarly, the *Roman Martyrology*, both in its traditional and revised (postconciliar) editions, includes an entry commemorating the prophet Job, whom some exegetes assume is an invented figure. Many other purportedly legendary OT figures are liturgically observed in the *Martyrology*.

12

The Canon

THIS SECTION IS NOT AN account of the historical process by which the canon of Scripture came to be defined, nor a defense of the place within the canon of any individual, controverted book. It sets forth, rather, general theological principles relevant to such historical and apologetical discussion.[140]

The Greek word "canon" (κανών) means a rod, originally one used for keeping something straight: by extension, it means any kind of rule or measure. "The doctrine of the apostles and prophets is called canonical, because it is a kind of rule for our understanding."[141] Here we use it in the narrower sense of the list of inspired books.

Not all the books inspired by the Holy Spirit are necessarily still extant. For example, "Solomon spoke three thousand parables: and his poems were a thousand and five" (3 Kings 4:32),

---

[140] For a summary of modern discussions on canonicity, see *The Canon Debate*, ed. Lee Martin McDonald and James A. Sanders (Grand Rapids: Baker Academic, 2002). This book, which contains essays by scholars of varying religious confessions, combines valuable historical scholarship with the groundless skepticism that mars much modern biblical exegesis.

[141] St Thomas Aquinas, *Commentary on the First Epistle of St Paul to Timothy*, ch. 1, lect. 1.

many more than have come down to us. The prophecy mentioned by St Matthew, that the Messias would be called a Nazarene (Matt. 2:23), is not clearly found in any earlier, known work.[142] St Paul, in the first letter to the Corinthians, says: "I wrote to you in an epistle not to keep company with fornicators" (1 Cor. 5:9), but the letter has not survived. In this sense, St Robert Bellarmine was able to say that "many truly sacred and canonical books have perished."[143]

Nevertheless, so much is Scripture a part of the inheritance of the Church militant that it would be audacious to suppose that any work had perished which God had antecedently willed to form an abiding part of His written word to man.[144] In this sense, we can say that the canon as willed by God contains seventy-two books, to which nothing can be added and from which nothing may be removed.

Under the Old Law, the canon was incomplete and perhaps uncertain. Incomplete, because the New Testament had not yet been written. Perhaps uncertain, since the fact that public divine revelation was still continuing means that there was no guarantee that God had revealed, as a truth to be held by all, the names of all the inspired and canonical books that had already been written.[145]

---

[142] It may, however, be St Matthew's summary of the passages in Isaiah and Zechariah where the Messiah is spoken of as a "branch," especially as he says that he is quoting from the prophet*s*, in the plural.

[143] *Controversiae*, "On the Word of God," Bk. IV, ch. 4.

[144] "Antecedently," i.e., as if He might have willed that such a book or passage of a book be part of His written word unless it was caused to perish by sin.

[145] Raymond Brown, after a survey of Jewish practice in Israel and Alexandria, and of the surviving evidence from Qumran, concludes that "there was no rigidly closed canon in Judaism in the first and early second centuries AD." Of Jews both in Alexandria and Israel it can be

Since public revelation ended with the death of the last apostle, the identity of the inspired books formed part of the apostolic preaching. For this reason, no book later than apostolic times, however excellent it may be, can be canonical:

> All later books are separated from the excellence of the canonical authority of the Old and New Testaments, which was confirmed in the times of the apostles and has come down through a continuous succession of bishops as the Church has spread, and, being set on high, claims the submission of every faithful and pious mind.[146]

On the other hand, none of the apostles, as far as we know, put into writing a divinely inspired list of the canonical books. John Calvin, to escape the conclusion that the word of God to man—in this case, His teaching about the identity of the inspired books—is in part unwritten, invented the idea that a book's property of "canonicity" can be known by a reader directly, as the tongue directly discerns sweet from bitter.[147] This doctrine,

said that "they had a large number of sacred books, some of which were recognized by all as older and more sacred than others": *New Jerome Biblical Commentary*, "Canonicity," 1041. My citation of this article is not an endorsement of its rationalist and modernist tendencies.

146 St Augustine, *Against Faustus*, Bk. 11, ch. 5.

147 *Institutes of the Christian Religion*, Bk. 1, ch. 7, 2: "Scripture bears upon the face of it as clear evidence of its truth, as white and black do of their color, sweet and bitter of their taste." Islam frequently offers a similar argument for the divine origin of Mohammed's Koran. More immediately, Calvin's claim was foreshadowed by Luther's insistence that Sacred Scripture is "most certain by means of itself, most easy, most obvious, its own interpreter, proving, judging, and enlightening all aspects of all matters ("ipsa per sese certissima, facillima, apertissima sui ipsius interpres, omnium omnia probans, iudicans, et illuminans"): from the preface of the *Assertio omnium articulorum*, published in 1521.

however, is to be found neither in Scripture itself nor in tradition. St Augustine's words to the Manichees are frequently and fitly quoted: "For my part, I should not believe the gospel except as moved by the authority of the Catholic Church (*Evangelio non crederem, nisi me Catholicae Ecclesiae commoveret auctoritas*)."[148] Commenting on this famous statement, Calvin claimed that St Augustine meant merely to say that he had originally come to believe in the gospel at the urging of some Catholic. Bellarmine refutes this claim by noting that the saint speaks of an obligation which binds him in the present, not in the past,[149] and that he speaks not of persuasion but of commands. For disputing with the Manichees about the reliability of their own scripture, which they were claiming was foreshadowed in the gospel, the bishop of Hippo says: "If you base yourself on the gospel, I shall base myself on those at whose command I believed the gospel; and at their bidding I shall in no way believe you."[150]

Nor is Calvin's doctrine of the self-evidence of canonicity compatible with experience: if it were true, there would be no place for discussion of the canonicity of a given book, nor even any need to practice textual criticism to discover which of the variant forms of a verse is the original, just as there is no need to discuss whether honey is sweeter or less sweet than lemon-juice, nor to take samples of each to a laboratory to discover the answer.

---

148 *Against the Fundamental Epistle of Manichaeus*, 6.

149 *Commoveret:* note that the imperfect subjunctive has present force in counter-factual statements.

150 "Si ad Evangelium te tenes, ego me ad eos teneam, quibus praecipientibus Evangelio credidi; et his iubentibus tibi omnino non credam." *Against the Fundamental Epistle of Manichaeus*, 6. For Bellarmine's commentary, see *Controversiae*, "On the Word of God," Bk. III.8.

No doubt sensing the weakness of his position, the tyrant of Geneva soon went on to assert that the sense by which canonicity is discerned does not in fact belong to all men, but only to those who are taught by the Holy Spirit,[151] that is, the elect, and only to these once they have been brought into the Church.[152] Yet this claim, even if it were otherwise plausible, would only shift and not solve his problem, for on Calvin's premises, one cannot identify the true Church until one has understood the Scriptures; but one cannot understand the Scriptures until one has identified them, which, on this view, one cannot do until one is in the true Church. On this view, a pagan adult cannot acquire knowledge of the Scriptures except by irrationally joining a church which he cannot know to be the true one.

In reality, while the Holy Spirit does assist a faithful reader of Scripture, for example to feel more keenly the relevance of some exhortation to his own life, or to discover some new interpretation of a parable, such graces reinforce the reader's prior acceptance of the inspired nature of the scriptural passage, and do not create this acceptance. Who, for example, would claim that he knew

---

[151] *Institutes of the Christian Religion*, Bk. 1, ch. 7, 5: "Those who are inwardly taught by the Holy Spirit acquiesce implicitly in Scripture. . . . Enlightened by him, we no longer believe, either on our own judgment or that of others, that the Scriptures are from God; but, in a way superior to human judgment, feel perfectly assured—as much so as if we beheld the divine image visibly impressed on it—that it came to us, by the instrumentality of men, from the very mouth of God."

[152] Ibid.: "This singular privilege God bestows on his elect only, whom he separates from the rest of mankind. . . . God having been pleased to reserve the treasure of intelligence for his children, no wonder that so much ignorance and stupidity is seen in the *generality* of mankind. In the generality, I include even those specially chosen, until they are ingrafted into the body of the Church."

solely "by the inward enlightenment of the Holy Spirit," rather than by the authority of accredited teachers, that the genealogies in the book of Chronicles, or the Mosaic permission to eat grasshoppers but not frogs' legs, were authentic Scripture?[153] Bellarmine therefore summarizes the Catholic doctrine on canonicity thus: "From the unwritten word of the apostles, passed down to us through the Church, we know what the written word of the apostles is."[154]

The books of the New Testament are called canonical not only in the sense that they were endorsed by the apostles, but also in that they have the apostles as their authors, or at least as their immediate overseers.[155] The Council of Trent, in a decree intended "to prevent any doubt from arising" about which are the canonical books, names the authors of all the New Testament books: it appears therefore to be no longer permissible to suggest, for example, that St John's Gospel or the Apocalypse was not written by the apostle John, or that the Epistle to the Hebrews was not written by St Paul.[156] It would also, as Bellarmine

---

[153] Fr Brian Harrison remarks: "He [Calvin] makes this preposterous claim that canonicity is self-evident for Spirit-led believers, not because he can offer any positive evidence for its truth, but simply because he is driven into this desperate corner by the exigencies of his polemic against Rome": "Logic and the Foundations of Protestantism," *Living Tradition* 18 (July 1988), www.rtforum.org/lt/lt18.html#II.

[154] *Controversiae*, "On the Word of God," Bk. IV, ch. 4.

[155] Summing up the principle that held sway in the Church from the beginning, Yves Congar wrote: "The principle of a canon is merely, and means simply, the principle of apostolicity": *Tradition and Traditions*, 39.

[156] *Dei Verbum* 18, by declaring that the four Gospels were written by the apostles themselves and by apostolic men, likewise excludes the claim that St Matthew's or St John's Gospel might not be the work of those two apostles. Bellarmine treats as heretical the claim that books of the New Testament were presented by their authors as the work of an

observes, be contrary to the way in which reasonable men judge of profane writings:

> If it is not sufficiently proved, by such a clear and continuous witness of so many centuries one after another, that the writings which the Church says and holds to have been propagated from the apostles, and spread far and wide through all nations, are indeed from the apostles, then the reliability of all writings and all books would necessarily be destroyed. For how do we know that the books of Hippocrates, Plato, Aristotle, Cicero, Varro and other such authors are really theirs? How is it that if someone denied that they were, he would be not only contradicted but laughed at, if not because from their time to ours they are witnessed to by an unbroken chain in such a way that one would have to be mad to put the matter in doubt?[157]

It may nonetheless be asked: if the contents of the canon of Scripture were part of the apostolic preaching, how was there room for debate on this subject among the Church Fathers, when there was no debate about subjects such as the Resurrection or Ascension? Here we may recall what was said above about truths which have always been necessary for all Christians to hold explicitly. The list of inspired books is not among these truths, and therefore the Holy Spirit did not have to supervise

apostle without truly being so: *Controversiae*, "On the Word of God," Bk. 1, ch. 6.

[157] Ibid. Manuscripts of New Testament works are, moreover, far more abundant than those of the works of profane authors. See L. de Blignières, *Christianity is Credible*, trans. Thomas Crean (Arouca Press: Bridgeport, 2022), 6–11.

the early development of the Church in such a way as to prevent any uncertainties on the subject from subsisting in the minds even of learned and holy bishops. It was sufficient, as Bellarmine notes, that from the earliest years of the Church, there were always men who could reliably testify which were the books that had come from the prophets and the apostles.[158] Yet it is true, as he adds, that the Church's readiness to define the canonicity of certain disputed books could and did increase over time. This increasing readiness, he explains, came from a recognition of the similarity of these books to the undisputed ones and from "the general sense and as it were the taste of the Christian people."[159] Yet neither the similarity of the disputed books to the undisputed ones nor the sense of the Christian people were the formal means by which the canonical nature of the books was known as revealed by God and definable: this formal means was, rather, their having been authenticated by the apostles. Hence, St Augustine, writing against Faustus, notes that whereas apocryphal books are so called because they derive from some unknown source and from the presumption of unknown men, the Church's judgement about the validity of her books is "supported by a succession of bishops from the original seats of the apostles up to the present time."[160]

[158] For this reason, he says, the "Book of Enoch" was never accepted, from lack of witnesses to testify to its origin.

[159] Ibid., ch. 10. He states that it is in this sense that St Jerome in *On Famous Men* could write that the Epistle of James gradually over the course of time acquired authority: "ex communi sensu, et quasi gustu populi Christiani, quomodo B. Hieronymus lib. de vir illus. in Jacobo dicit, epistolam Jacobi paulatim tempore procedente meruisse auctoritatem." St Jerome stated that not everyone accepted that this epistle was by St James. *On Famous Men* was written around 392.

[160] *Against Faustus*, Bk. 11, ch. 2.

At least from the fourth century, some local synods drew up official lists of the inspired books. Pope Innocent I, in a letter written in AD 405 to Exuperius, bishop of Toulouse, authoritatively declared which books were to be received.[161] The Council of Florence, in its *Decree for the Jacobites*, repeated the same list of inspired books. Nevertheless, at the time of the Council of Trent it was felt necessary to repeat the doctrine with the greatest possible weight, and so the canon was made the object of a dogmatic definition by that council on April 8, 1546, accompanied by an anathema.[162]

161 *PL* 20:501-2; DH 213. The same list is given in the *Decretum Damasi*, a record of the synod of Rome held under Pope Damasus I in 382. Scholars discuss whether some of this *Decretum* comes from a later period. See DH 178–80, with introductory note. Similar discussion exists about the *Decretum Gelasianum*, which also contains a list of the inspired books, and which is traditionally attributed to Pope Gelasius I (492–496).

162 DH 1502–4.

13

The Septuagint and the Vulgate

AMONG ALL THE TRANSLATIONS that have been made of the Scriptures, the Church has recognized two as possessing a special authority: the Greek version of the Old Testament known as the Septuagint, and the Latin Vulgate version.

The Septuagint

Since the New Covenant was not to be limited to the Jews, it was fitting and as it were necessary that a divinely-accredited version of the Old Testament exist which would be comprehensible to a large number of non-Jews in the first decades of the Church. Only thus could potential Gentile converts find assurance that Christ had fulfilled the promise and prophecies of the coming Redeemer; if such converts had had to rely on Jewish preachers speaking to them from Hebrew Scriptures which were unintelligible to them as non-Jews, they would doubtless have wondered whether the Scriptures truly said that which was ascribed to them by these preachers. Hence it was arranged by Divine Providence that the books of the Old Testament be translated into Greek, the common tongue of the whole Eastern empire, from the third century before Christ.[163] "This is how it came about, by a particular disposition of

[163] Congregation for Divine Worship and the Discipline of the Sacraments, *Fourth Instruction for the Right Application of the Conciliar Constitution on*

Providence, that not only those who heard Hebrew, but generally all peoples, were able to profit from our holy books."[164]

This version of Scripture is called the Septuagint, from the Latin word for "seventy" (*septuaginta*), the number or approximate number of its translators.[165] "The Church from the very beginning accepted as her own (*ut suam suscepit*) that very

the Liturgy (1994), no. 9: "The encounter between the Jewish world and Greek wisdom gave rise to a new form of inculturation: the translation of the Bible into Greek introduced the word of God into a world that had been closed to it and caused, under divine inspiration, an enrichment of the Scriptures."

[164] St John Chrysostom, *Homilies on Genesis*, 4.4. Not only Greek-speakers have benefitted from the Septuagint: for most of the history of the Western Church until the 1960s, and again today for an increasing number of clergy and religious, the Divine Office has mostly consisted of translations into Latin from the Greek psalter.

[165] Considerable obscurity lies over the origins of the Septuagint. The so-called *Letter of Aristeas*, which speaks of the translation made in the time of the Egyptian king Ptolemy Philadelphus (283–246 BC), mentions simply the Jewish *Law*, as St Jerome notes (*Commentary on Ezekiel*, ch. 5:12–13). Although this letter is generally held to date from the following century, it may nevertheless be correct in assigning the translation of the earliest books of the Bible to this period. In antiquity it was widely believed that the first translators had also converted the prophets and the other inspired writings into Greek. This is affirmed by Eusebius of Caesarea, among others, in the *Preparation of the Gospel*, VIII.1. Modern scholars, however, generally state that the remaining books of the Old Testament were translated in the course of the next two centuries. Nevertheless, the prologue to the book of Ecclesiasticus, dated around 130 BC, indicates that Greek versions of the prophets and the other writings were already in existence. Bellarmine points out in this connection that "Law" could be used by the Jews to refer to any of the sacred writings, as evidenced for example by Jn. 10:34 and 1 Cor. 14:21; *Controversiae*, "On the Word of God," 2.6. For further discussion, see Karen Jobbes and Moises Silva, *Invitation to the Septuagint* (Ada, MI: Baker Academic, 2015), 17–24.

ancient Greek translation of the Old Testament which is called the Septuagint."[166]

The translators of the Septuagint were held by the Fathers of the Church to have benefitted from an unusual degree of divine assistance, and to have in some way completed the work of the original Hebrew authors. St Irenaeus wrote that "the one and the same Spirit of God, who proclaimed by the prophets what and of what sort the advent of the Lord should be, did by these elders give a just interpretation of what had been truly prophesied."[167] "It was not alien to the inspiration of God, who gave the prophecy," wrote Clement of Alexandria, "also to produce the translation, and make it as it were Greek prophecy."[168] St Hilary spoke of the spiritual and heavenly knowledge which they possessed of the meaning of the psalms.[169] For his part, St Augustine wrote: "The same Spirit who was in the prophets, when they said these things, was also in those seventy men, when they translated them,"[170] and says that "all the more learned churches" recognize the presence and power of the Holy Spirit in this translation of the Scripture.[171] The bishop of Hippo maintained this position even while holding that they had not always translated literally, for example, by changing the "forty days" to "three days," in

---

[166] *Dei Verbum* 22.

[167] *Against the Heresies*, Bk. III.21.

[168] *Stromata*, Bk. I.22

[169] *On the Psalms*, preface; PL 9:238.

[170] *On the City of God*, Bk. XVIII.43. The authority of the Septuagint was eventually enshrined in Roman law itself, by the emperor Justinian in the law *De Hebraeis* (*novellum* 146) promulgated on February 8, 553.

[171] *De Doctrina Christiana*, Bk II.15. In the same place he mentions but does not vouch for the story that the translators independently produced the same version of the Scriptures. St Jerome treated this as a fable: see *Preface to the Pentateuch.*

Jonah's prophecy against Nineveh.[172] Bellarmine, summing up this tradition, claimed that "it must be taken as most certain that the seventy translators did their work excellently, with a particular assistance of the Holy Spirit, so that they would make no errors, and hence would seem to be not so much translators as prophets."[173] It seems that we should at least refer to the Septuagint as an "authentic" version of Scripture, in the sense of being instituted by God and guaranteed by Him to be a worthy version of the Old Testament.

The belief in the inspiration of the Septuagint is supported by the use which the apostles and Christ Himself made of it even when it does not correspond exactly to the Hebrew text as we now have it.

> Around the middle of the nineteenth century . . . D. M. Turpie made an extensive study of 275 NT passages and concluded that the NT, the LXX, and the MT[174] all agree in only about 20 percent of the quotations. Of the 80 percent where some disagreement occurs, less than 5 percent agree with the Hebrew against the LXX, while about a third of the quotations agree with the LXX against the Hebrew.[175]

---

[172] *On the City of God*, Bk. XVIII.44.

[173] *Controversiae*, "On the Word of God," bk. 2, ch. 6. John Lamont, alluding to a continuing discussion among theologians about the status of the Septuagint, writes: "This dispute is not over whether the Septuagint is an inspired translation of the Hebrew text (which it obviously is not, since there are substantial differences between the two). Rather, it is over whether the Septuagint *itself* is an inspired text": *Divine Faith*, 163–64.

[174] MT = Masoretic text, i.e., the Hebrew as we have it today.

[175] Forbes and Silva, *Invitation to the Septuagint*, 207. The authors note that such statistics are somewhat subjective, owing to the difficulty of

> Out of the thirty-seven quotations made by Jesus himself from the Old Testament, thirty-three agree almost *verbatim* with the LXX, two agree with the Hebrew and differ from the LXX, one differs from both, and one agrees partially with both. Only six agree exactly with the Hebrew.[176]

St Jerome, whom the liturgy celebrates as the "great explainer of sacred Scripture" (*in exponendis sacris Scripturi . . . Doctorem maximum*), defending himself against the charge of contempt for the Greek version of the Old Testament used by the Church, made a spirited rejoinder:

> Am I likely to have said anything derogatory to the seventy translators, whose work I carefully purged from corruptions and gave to Latin readers many years ago, and daily expound at our conventual gatherings; whose version of the psalms has so long been the subject of my meditation and my song? Was I so foolish as to wish to forget in old age what I learned in youth? All my treatises have been woven out of statements warranted by their version.[177]

Yet, as these words also indicate, St Jerome considered that the passage of time, and the influence of rival Greek versions on textual transmission, often made it difficult to be sure of the original Greek text. Although in his preface to his translation of

---

determining what counts as a quotation and what counts as "agreeing with."

[176] E.W. Grinfield, *An Apology for the Septuagint* (London: William Pickering, 1850), 30–31. The same author estimated (p. 90) that the number of direct quotations from the Greek Old Testament to be found in the New Testament occupy almost the same volume as St Mark's gospel. His book is marred in places by anti-Catholic polemic.

[177] *Apology against Rufinus*, Bk. II.24.

Chronicles/Paralipomenon, he observed that if we still possessed their version, his own work would be not needed, he states in his preface to Ezra that in fact "the variety of the texts shows them to be torn and perverted." Writing to Augustine, he explains that almost all the surviving Greek codices contain many additions from the translation made by Theodotion[178]: these additions had originally been separated from the Septuagint version by the use of asterisks, which had however been omitted by later copyists.[179] He also reported that the Jews themselves say that the Seventy, since they were writing for the benefit of gentiles, had removed certain things which could be misunderstood in favor of polytheism, and gives the example of a verse from the prophet Hosea, "Out of Egypt I called my son" (Hos. 11:1).[180] For such reasons, Bellarmine nevertheless considered that it is not safe in general to attempt to correct the Hebrew codices by means of the Greek,[181] nor did the Church do so when the Sixto-Clementine Vulgate was published in 1592. The extent to which it is possible today to establish from surviving manuscripts and ancient quotations the Greek version of the Old Testament produced by its first translators remains a controversial and complex subject.[182]

---

[178] Theodotion is traditionally thought to have been a convert to Judaism who lived in the late second century after Christ.

[179] Listed as Letter 75 in the letters of St Augustine, ch. 5.

[180] *Preface to the Pentateuch*, quoted also in his *Apology against Rufinus*, Book II.24.

[181] *Controversiae*, "On the Word of God," bk. 2, ch. 6.

[182] See Jobbes and Silvas, *Invitation to the Septuagint*, 34–62, for an account of some of the complexities of the textual transmission, and 129–47 for the modern scholarly debate about the proper aims of biblical textual criticism. These authors maintain (p. 134) that reconstruction of the primitive Greek text is "a legitimate and necessary enterprise." The Septuaginta-Unternehmen center in Göttingen has produced critical

The Vulgate

> The Hebrews had an authentic Scripture in their language; the Greeks also had an authentic Greek Scripture, that is, the Old Testament in the Septuagint version, and the first sources of the New Testament; so it was right that the Latin Church, in which is the see of Peter, and in which the Christian faith was to remain in perpetuity, should have an authentic Scripture in its language.[183]

This authentic Latin version of Sacred Scripture is the Vulgate (the term comes from the Latin word *vulgata*, "published," and hence, "commonly available"). It is not entirely the work of St Jerome, but he is more responsible for it than any other one man.

> The term "Vulgate" normally means the Latin Bible that has been in common use in the Western Church since the seventh century. This Bible is not the work of one author: nor is it the product of any one age. It is a collection of translations which differ both in origin and in character. In the Old Testament, most books are Jerome's translations made from the Hebrew; but the Psalter is an Old-Latin[184] text which was corrected by Jerome to agree with the Greek text of Origen's Hexapla, while some books (Wisdom,

editions of the Pentateuch, all the prophets, and most of the deutero-canonical books: *Septuaginta: Vetus Testamentum Graecum* (Göttingen: Vandenhoeck & Ruprecht, 1936–). This work supersedes the provisional critical edition produced by Alfred Rahlfs in the 1930s.

[183] *Controversiae*, "On the Word of God," bk. 2, ch. 10.

[184] The Old Latin (also called the *Vetus Latina* or the *Itala*) is "an early translation of the Greek Bible into Latin . . . produced as early as the second century of our era"; Jobbes and Silva, *Invitation to the Septuagint*, 373. The translator or translators who produced it are unknown.

> Ecclesiasticus, Baruch, and Maccabees) are pure Old-Latin and untouched by Jerome. In the New Testament, all the books have an Old-Latin base; but this base has been revised in the light of the Greek with varying degrees of thoroughness—in the Gospels rather hurriedly, in most other books more carefully. The reviser of the Gospels was certainly Jerome: the reviser(s) of the other books, or groups of books, are altogether unknown. The Vulgate, therefore, is far from being a unity, and the only justification for calling it "Jerome's Vulgate" (as we often do) is that there is more of his work in it than there is of anyone else's.[185]

For Bellarmine, the authority of the Vulgate may be discerned first of all from history:

> Not by mere haphazard [*temere*] has the whole Latin Church used this version alone for about a thousand years, that is, from the time of Blessed Gregory; nor by mere haphazard have all preachers explained this version and put it before the peoples, and all councils brought forth evidence from it to establish the dogmas of the faith.[186]

The Church would have been badly provided for, continues the same author, if she had not possessed an authentic Latin version

[185] *Biblia Sacra iuxta Vulgatam Versionem*, ed. B. Fischer et al. (Stuttgart: Deutsche Bibelgesellschaft, 1994), Preface to the first edition (1969), xxix. This work is "an edition which reflects the original text [of the Vulgate] as precisely as possible"; ibid., Preface to fourth edition, xxxiv. It should not be confused with the neo-Vulgate Bible (*Nova Vulgata*), which is a fresh translation into Latin of the Hebrew Old Testament and the Greek New Testament, and which was published by order of Pope John Paul II in 1979.

[186] *Controversiae*, "On the Word of God," Bk. 2, ch. 10..

to refer to in her councils, since few or no bishops read Hebrew, and there was a time when few or none knew Greek.

While inspiration has not generally been claimed for the Vulgate, we may therefore say that it is, like the Septuagint, of divine *institution*; since the Church is governed by the Spirit of truth, the prevalence of the Vulgate from the patristic era onwards shows sufficiently that it is a reliable expression of the written word of God. The Council of Trent, therefore, in declaring the Vulgate "authentic" (*authenticum*) was not simply establishing a fact but recognizing one.[187] The declaration implies principally that the Vulgate contains no errors in faith or morals, and secondly, according to Bellarmine, that it contains no deliberate falsification or "obvious deformity."[188] He adds that it is still good to read the Scriptures in Hebrew and Greek, as he did himself, since even an authentic translation does not necessarily possess "all the clarity, all the force, and all the connotations of the original text."[189]

While the Church could in the future declare some other translation of the Scriptures to be also "authentic," she does not

---

[187] Session IV: "The same sacred and holy Synod, considering that no small utility may accrue to the Church of God, if it be made known which out of all the Latin editions, now in circulation, of the sacred books, is to be held as authentic, ordains and declares, that the said old and vulgate edition, which, by the lengthened usage of so many years, has been approved of in the Church, be, in public lectures, disputations, sermons and expositions, held as authentic; and that no one is to dare or presume to reject it under any pretext whatever."

[188] *Vindiciae*, de Verbo Dei, bk. 2, ad cap. 7. It leaves open the question of whether a better translation of this or that phrase would be possible; he gives the example of whether some Hebrew word for a particular species of tree or animal could be more accurately rendered.

[189] Ibid.: "omnem claritatem, omnem energiam, omnes allusiones textus originalis."

have the power to "de-authenticate" either the Septuagint or the Vulgate, if these versions are indeed of divine institution. Again, unless circumstances should ever arise in the Church in which some translation other than the Septuagint or the Vulgate prevails for an extended period as the only one which can be known and understood by the bishops, there will not again be the possibility for the Church to recognize that some translation is vouched for by the Holy Spirit. Hence, if the Church ever declared some future version authentic, she would not then be recognizing but rather creating, even if infallibly, this authenticity. "In these three languages especially is the mystery of God's will preached, and the expectation of the blessed kingdom."[190]

[190] St Hilary, *Commentary on the Psalms*, preface: "His maxime tribus linguis Sacramentum voluntatis Dei, et beati regni expectation praedicatur."

Selected Bibliography and Further Reading

Magisterium

Council of Trent, Session IV, *Decree on Sacred Books and Traditions*

Pope Leo XIII, Encyclical Letter *Providentissimus Deus*

Pope Pius XII, Encyclical Letter *Divino Afflante Spiritu*

Second Vatican Council, Dogmatic Constitution on Divine Revelation *Dei Verbum*

Doctors of the Church

St Augustine, *De Doctrina Christiana* ("On Christian Doctrine")

St Thomas Aquinas, *Summa Theologiae*, I, Q. 1; *Quaestiones Quodlibetales*, VII, question 6

St Robert Bellarmine, *Controversiae*, "On the Word of God," books 1–4

Secondary Sources

Dictionnaire de Théologie Catholique. Paris: Letouzey & Ané, 1907–51. Articles "Canon des Livres Saints"; "Écriture Sainte"; "Inspiration de l'Écriture."

Billot, Louis. *De Inspiratione sacrae Scripturae*. Rome: St Joseph's Press, 1906.

Boyle, John. *Aquinas on Scripture: A Primer.* Steubenville, OH: Emmaus Academic, 2023.

Chalk, Casey. *The Obscurity of Scripture: Disputing* Sola Scriptura *and the Protestant Notion of Biblical Perspicuity*. Steubenville, OH: Emmaus Road, 2023.

Feingold, Lawrence. *Faith Comes from What Is Heard: An Introduction to Fundamental Theology*. Steubenville, OH: Emmaus Academic, 2016.

Hahn, Scott, and Benjamin Wiker. *Politicizing the Bible: The Roots of Historical Criticism and the Secularization of Scripture 1300–1700*. New York: Herder & Herder, 2013.

Harrison, Brian. "Does Vatican Council II Allow for Errors in Sacred Scripture?" *Living Tradition*, March–May 2010.

Holmes, Jeremy. *Cur Deus Verba: Why the Word Became Words*. San Francisco: Ignatius Press, 2021.

Jobbes, Karen, and Moises Silva. *Invitation to the Septuagint*. Ada, MI: Baker Academic, 2015.

Kwasniewski, Peter. "The Inspiration and Inerrancy of Sacred Scripture." *OnePeterFive*, February 22, 2023. https://onepeterfive.com/inerrancy-sacred-scripture/.

Lamont, John. *Divine Faith*. Routledge: New York and London, 2016.

Nicolau, Miguel. "On Sacred Scripture." *Sacrae Theologiae Summa* 1B [1958]. Translated by Kenneth Baker, SJ. Saddle River, NJ: Keep the Faith, n.d.

You might enjoy some other titles published by Os Justi Press:

Dogmatic Theology

Lattey (ed.), *The Incarnation*
Lattey (ed.), *St Thomas Aquinas*
Pohle, *God: His Knowability, Essence, and Attributes*
Pohle, *The Author of Nature and the Supernatural*
Scheeben, *A Manual of Catholic Theology* (2 vols.)
Scheeben, *Nature and Grace*

Spiritual Theology

Doyle, *Vocations*
Guardini, *Sacred Signs*
Leen, *The True Vine and Its Branches*
Swizdor, *God in Me*

Liturgy

A Benedictine Martyrology
The Life of Worship
The Roman Martyrology (Pocket Edition)
Chaignon, *The Sacrifice of the Mass Worthily Offered*
Croegaert, *The Mass: A Liturgical Commentary* (2 vols.)
Kwasniewski (ed.), *John Henry Newman on Worship, Reverence, and Ritual*
Parsch, *The Breviary Explained*
Pothier, *Cantus Mariales*
Shaw, *Sacred and Great*

Language & Literature

The Little Flowers of Saint Francis (illustrated)
Brittain, *Latin in Church*
Farrow, *Pageant of the Popes*
Kilmer, *Anthology of Catholic Poets*
Lazu Kmita, *The Island Without Seasons*
Papini, *Gog*
Walsh, *The Catholic Anthology*

Printed in Great Britain
by Amazon

27033972R00057